JOHN A. SCOTT

ST CLAIR

THREE NARRATIVES

ABOUT *UNTAPPED*

Most Australian books ever written have fallen out of print and become unavailable for purchase or loan from libraries. This includes important local and national histories, biographies and memoirs, beloved children's titles, and even winners of glittering literary prizes such as the Miles Franklin Literary Award.

Supported by funding from state and territory libraries, philanthropists and the Australian Research Council, *Untapped* is identifying Australia's culturally important lost books, digitising them, and promoting them to new generations of readers. As well as providing access to lost books and a new source of revenue for their writers, the *Untapped* collaboration is supporting new research into the economic value of authors' reversion rights and book promotion by libraries, and the relationship between library lending and digital book sales. The results will feed into public policy discussions about how we can better support Australian authors, readers and culture.

See untapped.org.au for more information, including a full list of project partners and rediscovered books.

Readers are reminded that these books are products of their time. Some may contain language or reflect views that might now be found offensive or inappropriate.

For Kathryn Riessen, Robert Moore
and Steve Dunne

CONTENTS

Run in the Stocking

Acknowledgments

The description of the lavatories in Part 13 of *St Clair* is based on writings of Leonid Plyushch, detained in Dnepropetrovsk Special Psychiatric Hospital from 1973-76. Warren's "notes" in Part 16 are based on a statement made by Superintendent Odezhkin to dissident Yurii Belov at the Psychiatric Hospital of Poimo-Tiny, Krasnoyarsk Territory and Superintendent Rubashov's diagnosis of demonstrator Valentin Ivanov at Psychiatric Hospital No. 7, Institutskii Lane 5, Moscow.

St Clair was awarded the 1984 Mattara Poetry prize. It appeared as part of the 1984 Mattara Anthology, *Neither Nuked nor Crucified* (ed. Christopher Pollnitz) and was reprinted in *Scripsi* magazine.

Preface was written as part of a one-year Writer's Fellowship from the Literature Board of the Australia Council. The versions of *Catullus 63* and *Propertius II, 26a* are based on plain prose translations by Michael Heyward.

My thanks go to John Garnett for providing me with a home and good company whilst in Melbourne; to John Croyston of the ABC for his help in turning *Run in the Stocking* and *St Clair* into television drama; and in particular to Martin Duwell for his continued faith in, and support of, my writing.

PREFACE

for Helen Williams of Ainslie
'if she wants it'

Only what prepares it, only what destroys it can be told.

Gide, *The Immoralist*

And if I speak to you outside of what I have written, these marginal comments cannot have the value of what I have written, these marginal comments cannot have the value of the work itself.

Hegel, 'Preface' to the *Phenomenology of the Mind*

What is not herein described must be guessed.

Spare, *The Grimoire of Zos*

1 Sydney

Only what prepares it. Novel. Arcana. By five I had stared five hours across these leaves of paper — misbegotten — stared at pencil shavings, curled and broken from a sharpener, coned upon the desk like tiny lampshades. Light begetting light. Morning smoothing out the harsher shadows of my face as a caring maid might deal with sheets.

Carl dead? An improbable end. Improbable that such an easy solution might come to pass. "It" was dead, we knew that; Carl perhaps most of all: these last temptations finished or completed. I would say "surely", for surely that word is to me so much a part of my memory, of the Bible ——— ("Surely": the way doubt has crept into the word) and yes, surely this city is a desert.

Too late he journeyed, as his father before him, for heat. For that unbearable overcoat skin of heat: temperature and the claret odour of mating.

But then the first traffic was calling its devotion through an undisturbed air. Only what prepares it; what destroys it. As preface and *postscriptum* are, presently, this single thought.

Once, around the walls of Gus' bed-sitter, were several of his early water-colours; and here a delicate gouache; paths that bent beyond sight — dirt wrists fallen to the arms of heavy furniture — Alfred Sisley's road to Sèvres; that told the ease with which a life might be brutalized quite casually by circumstance.

But why have I chosen to start these meditations with a character who plays no part within the narrative? Improbable beginning!

'Call me,' Julia added, her goodbyes desperate or inviting 'or write, or something . . .'

But let me start at the end. These last days of Carl. Days before he left. Before I learnt another man's solitude, and could choose another mask, if I chose, on the streets of ordeal — my life, characterized by a willing sadness, undetected amidst this crowd-seclusion; buffeted or ignored — no matter.

Those days *Passacaglia's* ate with an open mouth. I would sit amongst that wailing-wall of tweed — these "scribblers'" coats — their suede patches mopping at the spillage on the bar.

The gods had condemned him to endless drinking. His entrance, marked by a desultory admission that to come here again, as he always came, was defeat.

'Scotch on the rocks, sir?'

He took his drink — the struggle towards the heights was enough to fill a man's heart — its ponderous weight rolling in his mouth; he felt it career wildly down the mountainside of his throat.

'Same again, sir?'

One must imagine Carl happy.

You see, I could apply that comic metaphor to our search: simply at the point of emergence, love reverts to loss.

'I remember Peter saying that once you'd had a woman, she wasn't the same. From then on you knew you could always have her.'

So Carl talked. In his hand a volume of Rilke, and Rilke's face like the Christ of the Protestant Bible.

'He was making a film about the martial arts at the time. On his humble way to stardom. Jealousy's a dreadful curse, you know.' He paused. 'You don't suppose, I mean, they're not back together?'

Those nights, the bar was a colony of defence. Mirrors filled with the idea of women, smeared on the loose florid wounds of our faces.

'I once bought her a pendant. Her initial in silver. I remember her saying I'd have to call her Hester from now on. She said it was a licence to continue in her life without deception, and without guilt. Do you see her?'

I shook my head.

'You know Yeats once said that rhetoric comes from the quarrel with others, and poetry from the quarrel with ourselves . . .'

He responded to some change of expression I was unaware of having made.

'I haven't memorized it or anything. It's quoted in the Introduction.'

He dropped the book. Our Lord of the spilling. Our Lord of drunkenness.

And at the end. His face with all its surface noise. A too familiar record with a hiss of thirties jazz; its jumping and its scratches; and its sticking, its accursed sticking.

Carl Explains His Love of a Girl Named Sandy

'I was breathing her. Inhaling the powder of her. And her hair had the odour of smoke. No, the odour of sun-heated newspapers.'

Carl Explains His Need for Alcohol

'O God, in case of sex! To excuse myself. You know how much I fear impotence. Horridly, *horribly,* sorry. Impotence. And all the derision of impotence. You see I can say it was the scotch, you see. A curse brought down on all from gatekeepers onwards.

Actually you know, I'm so relieved when they're gone. When I'm left to the safety of my desire for them.'

Carl Explaining Sex

'Carl my dear, makes love with difficulty. His strength falls to the sheets; his arms cannot support such a disarray of flesh. His imagination is cheated by the women who might drop to his bed *entre deux boissons.* He is cheated out of fantasies he dare not admit on a first occasion. And he is cheated by their failure to return! He can, at least, laugh about it!'

Cynthia Goes to Brighton
from Propertius II, 26a

She drowns upon this
charmed *muezzin* afternoon. The calls go out
from Neptune's Cave: *Cast off 'is bollocks!*
as the latest sea-blanched suicide is netted
for the evening news. But Cynthia's legs have
touched a nerve. The rheumy eyes of Mr G.,
aquarium owner, start to clear. A canine shift,
a scratch. Across the pier his sisters bitch
in tête-à-tête of sinuses and nausea.
Down at the Marina, a dolphin noses
sex-dolls from the pool. It's time to put
the opera glasses down. Our view collapses
from the Ferris wheel to beach as, terrified,
we iris into black, and wake.

Carl Brouwer, December 1981

Can any writing achieve love? Redeem it from indifference? And what might it do when sent on such a mission? What story does it tell?

Or only when everyone it has ever met and ever spoken to is assembled together in this single room to compare stories, only then do you realize the extent of the lie?

'Do you remember our last dinner here?'

I did. That final night in Sydney, two years before, when I had left the bar with Julia, through a stifling summer rain, into her crowded namesake restaurant. 'Two years ago. I thought I'd never see you again.' We had both eventually finished this half-finished meal — but she had purposefully kept apart her knife and fork: a displacement that was simply a request for silence.

'I hated you that night.'

I thought of telling her by way of confirmation how much I had quite reasonably hated myself — of trying to suggest it was no longer so — but the cutlery remained censorious.

'You were such a dreadful stranger. Pushing everyone away. Like him.' She edged the knife. 'And I told you about Carl's photographs, didn't I. Yes?'

And I agreed, but she pursued the memory no further. Only sat more properly in her high-backed chair beneath that single decorator gull, and continued I remember in the strict metre of a ballad.

'He left here shortly after that. In March of Eighty-two. He wrote a letter to me, every month. Eighteen letters, quite regularly.'

'Woman's curse.'

'And then, four months ago, they simply stopped. You see, I never actually *read* any of them. I couldn't bear to. I knew they'd be full of blackmail and history and *her.* But then I never expected them to stop.'

She reached below the table for her bag — and I, instinctively offering her a lighted match — and placed the letters on the table.

Let me be quite clear: at first I thought this was to be a narrative concerning several letters sent by Carl to Julia. It was to be about her fear; who could no more open those letters than re-live the seven years that in part occasioned them. And when they had no longer come ...

'I want *you* to read them,' Julia said. 'No, please. Find out what happened to him. Why he might've stopped. Only you see, I don't want you to tell me. All I want to know is whether — for whatever reason — I could have borne to read what's written in them. Not what they say, you understand. A "Yes" or a "No".'

His letters, tied with dark blue ribbon (navy), sat between our plates, our inappropriate meal, her knife and fork together.

'Call me,' she said, leaving two ten dollar notes she must have gathered with the letters, 'or write, or something . . .'

And more obviously, at reading what another could not bear; becoming on those eighteen occasions someone else, un-sexed, un-timed; about the fear within myself.

These remarkable faces are blue-black
    they are bruised and torn
A writing forced into every corner of the page
    pressed against the very margins of the world
Asylum letters brought from Northampton
    starved of space
Warehouse letters brought from Amsterdam
    starved of time

And these other faces
    scored and stitched
These words that stare through
    the bars of deletion
Behind this fence
Behind these barricades
Behind this last familiar border
    that are displayed here
    that are condemned here
And what earlier remarks obliterated
    in some cases almost completely through the page
How many words in these inescapable complicities?
And what of these others that walk amongst us
    that parade their filthy eloquence
What bargain will they have struck
    to so live?

Extracts from March 1982 letter

Dear Julia,

I write as always, my confessor, during these times when to see you might put our appearances between the truth. How the letter is written in a certain knowledge of concealment. An utterance that we fold and cover, that we enclose and seal; it is surely for that "other" only: breaker of the seals. What might we say, knowing they would be made public! Very little I suspect. . . . .

How many years ago she touched me, saying: *On y va! My body is a map. This country in the perfect shape of your desire. Go there! Exhaust this inexhaustible longing. Start this journey's end. There amongst the dull exhausted dogs of refuse; there amongst the stench of open sewers; the rot-*

ting flesh of the tanneries. Go there! Kiss the dark sex of this place. Infidel. Despised of the savage moon!

Carl.

I can, I believe, remember her saying these words — whispered or declaimed — if not to him . . .

2 Fès

from April, 1982

A savage charge. A raw stutter of single-shot rifles: late afternoon of the *Mousseum.* Nomadic horsemen proclaiming their skill and sex beyond the city walls.

I am born again. Of fire and noise, and these impossible children, I had forgotten. I spoke in tongues to distance them — all except Majid, who called to me in English, as if already well aware of my destination. . . . .

Walls polished by passing animals, rubbed down to the herringbone of another age. Day of the million donkeys. Cobbled paths and alleyways; stalls of dead owls and jackal-feet. . . . .

I was trapped by the closing of district gates. A sudden rush of metal; wood-snort hard on wood. All timber here possessed by arab horses. Mane-shavings. . . . .

Hurrying after midnight to my hotel through the ghosted trenches of these alleyways, street-lights in approaching quarters seemed to vanish. Behind me, blinking awake. As if some natural force had sought to keep me from the light. No doubt coincidence of power failure: a radio, a lamp too much, switched on, perhaps occasioned by my passing. . . . .

from May, 1982

Majid introduced me to Aosman. What an extraordinary description I would have to make of him: as if one were looking at a personhl from two different places at the same time. Clearly a mesmerism of his peculiar device used upon strangers at the time of introduction. . . . .

Aosman, who must have been a young man here in the 1930s, lives with a black-haired girl called Zora. Lithe, in her mid-twenties, possibly younger, she moves about the house as if she were blind, yet guided perfectly by some unseen hand. . . . .

Like all beautiful women, she manifests many of the characteristics of animals: a tendency to flight; an almost imperceptible dilation of the nostrils at the approach of others; a whiplash of regard as if the most innocuous stranger might become a threat.

I imagine Zora reincarnated of the gazelle or the pony: a grace or awkwardness; a body that is "carried" by its legs. . . . .

Over mint tea, we spoke of *The Moroccans* of Matisse — mosque or melon bodies; a fleshing architecture; fruit that prays on mats of wire — all embraces all.

When Aosman momentarily left the room, Zora turned her cup face-down upon the table.

'Today you fascinate me,' she said.

And as I smiled, the cup parrot-squealed across the glass beneath the *séance* of her sight. . . . .

Zora and Aosman dancing to Bowlly's *Isn't it Heavenly* along the upstairs balcony. He, an old man, shuffling; pushed almost like a chess-piece across the tiles . . . "to be so romantically and frantically in love with you" . . . as the sea-voiced palms split into a thousand daggers, stabbing at the night.

No doubt this place encourages these constant murders: most obviously the maze of the medina that draws you within, until night. And who will lead you out then for any price, which is now simply there for the taking.

For this we can prepare. No, it is always openness that catches us unawares; that destroys us. Trees bend to kiss us and then . . .

'I do not think she is for you,' continued Aosman, 'despite your evident desire.'

I began a pointless protest.

'Do have some more gin; my favourite spirit. That's a joke here of course, yes? Ah, we have so much to talk about; much use to which to put our language and our thoughts.'

He paused, his gestures frozen to a statue precision that encouraged no reply, as if speech were somehow prerequisite for motion; then continued, sinking back into his chair.

'Why do you desire Zora? She is not perfect for you as she is for me. Is it then because you simply wish a body? Or because she touches you? Or touches me?'. . . . .

from June, 1982

Perhaps I was ensnared by this forbidden alcohol: my mind revolving on those Bill Evans songs. Piano. Forte. Jazz.

Aosman suggested that I leave the hotel and take up residence in his villa. . . . .

The following Wednesday we were joined by a young Art student who had much to say about finding oneself through dance. He described in terminal detail the difficulties of block-and-tackling a grand piano up a misty hillside in New Hampshire so that an unsuspecting and perfectly innocent sunrise might be welcomed by Debussy and a Gurdjieff gavotte!

Later that night as a "gift" he performed (unaccompanied) an Assyrian warrior breathing dance. Nevertheless this seemed to impress Zora who declared him "special" in our company.

Shortly after both had announced their "tiredness", I caught a glimpse of him moving into her room. So be it. He had travelled much in the land of the free and the home of the brave.

Aosman and I remained awake — the single shafts of perfumed smoke columning to heaven. I wondered how he might abide the humiliation of this present circumstance.

We listened to another jazz till dawn: Lennie Tristano — a hiss under breath and a surface noise. Keyboard air.

At one point Zora's screams could be heard quite clearly, counterpointed against the music. Only then Aosman brought himself to speak:

'Beauty is too simple,' he said. 'And you surely cannot begrudge our young man; crippled as he is by that Apollonian gaze.'. . . .

from July, 1982

'These questions that you ask,' Aosman interjected. 'The possessive idealize love: and thus, the morbid awakening.'

Holding the large globe ashtray in his hand, he sat in the Hoffman chair beneath an ancient tapestry: distant mountains guarded by a rams' head border.

'Now if you take the ugly,' he continued, 'or the deformed, or the old, and transcend your natural revulsion by uniting with it aesthetically — sometimes even physically — a rare ecstasy results which generates great magical potential.' And he gently blew a pencil-line of smoke, I presume from the cigarette I never saw him once inhale. . ..

from August, 1982

'You are still too pure. You are still full of moral prejudice and conformity. Your mind and your desire must become amoral. Focussed. Able to accept everything. Before it can control, the life force must be free of every inhibition. Now you must kiss me goodnight.' Leaning forward to Aosman's hand, I felt his long scarlet fingernails bite into my palm. When I looked up, he was smiling; his teeth almost transparent with the years of cheap tobacco.

'I shall prepare you a sigil,' he said, 'to satisfy these energies you squander on Zora.'. . . .

On Thursday, Aosman called me to his study. I found him as usual behind that barricade of leather-bound books. On the oak table before him lay several sheets of paper covered with black letter-markings.

'Now, we must symbolize desire and give it form. Here you see, I have embodied the letters of her name into this single sign: the comprehensible focus of her essence.'

The armoured insects of these designs swarmed across the pages; their lettered thorns; their barbed wire of word.

'And now,' he said, 'we must wait.'. . . . .

from September, 1982

Night. Moist and thickening air. Exquisite plumage of wind. Waves breaking through the room. At two I was awakened by Aosman, gently grasping my shoulder.

'She is here, my friend,' he said.

I turned towards the door, only to see it close. I turned back to Aosman to find him gone. I span my head back to the door, now open.

'Carl,' I heard behind me.

I turned towards this woman's voice, the door closing behind me. I could see her body: only glints of proportion, moon-sabred through palm. I saw scythes of eye-lash hair that grew high on her belly and breasts: black harvest. Silver harvest. I moved towards the candle.

'No!' she cried.

I realized how fire might frighten her, like any animal. Her body was beside me, as if it were beneath an armour of lids; as if the whole flesh of her might suddenly awake, opening into a thousand eyes.

'Did Aosman pay for you?' I asked.

'If you wish me to leave . . .' And she swung suddenly from the bed and stood above me.

'No.'

I caught a crescent glimpse of soaking hair, matted to her inner thigh. She was watching me between these darknesses.

'Why do you touch yourself?' she asked. 'All men seem

to touch themselves before sex. There is no need. There is nothing you can do to yourself that I cannot do to you. Do I worry you? Do I frighten you with my appearance? Of course. How unlikely I must seem.'

Palm-light. Waves that broke upon her arms.

'Come,' she said. 'Feed me. Silence me.'. . . . .

I broke and persisted in my breach: her warbled cry spitting back across my genitals. I felt my body jolted backwards, punched as if by an immense surge of electricity; my leg doubling beneath me.

As I lay there, immobile, a massive winged figure seemed to move above me, and in a wild frenzy of derisive flapping, shambled through the opening door and was gone.

For the next three days I was confined to bed, in fever — infected no doubt by this prostitute.

I imagined Aosman visited (as of course he must; or was a constant presence?) throwing his keys against my pillow, like skeleton fingers crossed before me, saying:

'I am sorry for her sudden departure. She was simply terrified by the force of your desire. Yet even now you must understand how the force itself has rapidly diminished. For instance, would you now bother claiming her as yours?'. . . . .

from October, 1982

Dear Julia,

Just then, your name. I had forgotten. And now your presence strong as jasmine. Who have you become in this silence? And, so close, how shall you find me, perhaps forced into these lies of compensation; our two lives so far, so secret.

How suddenly this necessity to tell you of those affairs during our last two years. To ask if perhaps you knew, suspected any of this? And how much I may have feared, or longed for the suspicion of others. Of course, in no way do I wish the sharing of these hidden truths to obligate you. When I speak to you of love, you are no more bound than before. If that is possible. . . . .

from November, 1982

The dark eyes of these children, their abyss: young girls gathered at the boundary of their *menarche.*

And this child — Ginette — the simple appearance of an un-sexed boy. I run my hands down her brown hipless thighs. Everything — exclude the leather of the feet — a buttered smoothness; everything a pouting. A sex at first emergence. Everywhere this slight swelling. . . . .

I watch the townspeople as we pass: watch them hold aloft their whitened hands to ward me away. I smell them burn their stupid piles of dung; their dead animals.

One day Ginette arrived, her hair the odour of burnt feathers: prepared by her family for our assignations. And surely they must have known (my fine-boned child) how I asked nothing of her I had not done myself a hundred times whilst *being* her. . . . .

My time here dies. I leave for England to bring myself to her. As her time also draws near.

I journey to my bride. More various. More complete. How familiarity chokes the known and saps the force of life; induces that "fatigue-indifference" of which my Aosman spoke.

The truest whore-writing must be infinite. Inexperienced. Yes, for the pornographic, how the "writing" ultimately kills the "whore".

Carl.

3 London

A writing, as we know, cannot intend. And yet I come increasingly to the view that it may be possible for writing to have an inadvertence so deliberate that, for instance, one might reasonably speak of "the inadvertence to arouse". "Assassin sex", as Carl might say, and I no less an addict — with our fatal attraction to the destructive — chained with the perfumed hair of night.

How implicated I become.
How the very act of reproduction
makes pornography out of silence.
How inadvertently I have enjoined you
to become another reader.
How together we shall make these letters
objects of arousal.
How they shall arouse again
(if only) through us.

As inadvertently
every writing is pornography, every speech
an admission of a crime of sex.
As inadvertently
we prostitute this "woman-thought" through our
descriptions and use our words as whores.
As inadvertently
we create our fictions in the sexual act.

As Gus, who has left his Asian child-bride for a holiday in this city, might see cunnilingus as a form of confession.

from December, 1982

I have entered them — their paste-flesh marbled with stretch marks — my filthy mothers, with my foot or forearm massaged in the black grease of a channel swimmer; and in their ecstasies have heard them bellow, roused oblivious:

'O, lovey, oooh that great big cock of yours!'

I have poured their lust — these hags of every possible extremity — into this single mould. Each night I breathe more life; each night I shape the words by which she shall be known; her true description, chartered, quartered: angel in her latitudes of flesh.

I watch the fearsome animations of this single room: the time-lapse shutterings, dusk-blink, moon-degrees, building nests across my face with twigs of light. Rustlings. Papers; drawings thoroughly disturbed by wind: their outlines smudged by breath to smoke; the ink bleeding upwards through the air like myriad veins of black-bird feet, death stiffened. Multitude. (A murder of crows). . . . .

Where is this place? This hazing planet, corrugated by the wind; these oases, iris-stained; these whitened yod-seeds blowing, breaking from the sun.

What animal laps at these dark saucers; hears the soft moons brushing in catastrophe? Black flame and brown luminescence. Dark salt of flesh that runs between the pyramids of day and night.

Where is this shore, knotted with material, hem and ledge. What gristle-animal burrows there. What horse approaches, prepared by such saddles. And who is this other: calling creatures unto him, begging to be silenced; this hermit cloaked in suffering — shirt, hood and blood? . . . .

from January, 1983

My filthy Winifred has taken me to mass. My Winifred has led me to my followers.

I kissed these naked children, their genitals ablaze with silver rings. I moved amongst them at their rituals. And they in turn saw rain fall from my open palms; they saw me rise above them, saw me cast myself down from the altar and these angels bear me up.

Winifred's Tale

'It should've shattered, but the glass broke with this single chime, like a doorbell. The curtains came apart and this huge winged animal — big as a cow — flew in, hooked me with its claws and took me off over the rooftops like Peter bloody Pan! I was pissing myself; God help 'em below, I suppose!

Well it carried me right down to the dockyards, and I thought, the bloody thing'll take me off to sea. So I squirmed and screamed blue murder, until it let go and I dropped backwards on the altar here.

Anyway, I told them what had happened, and we went out to the window. It was all frosted over on account of the cold, and in the frost you could see all these claw marks; and on the ledge this stuff that smelt like dead fish. And it was still moving, like it could breathe.'. . . . .

Brian took me up to see his urchins: the car-struck animals he's collecting for a one-man show. A mummified cat — two feet of grin; a sparrow — the body peeled backwards from the beak like fruit; a stole of something.

He is also the leader of a rock group I intend to manage: their music presently a bleak persistent bass on which hangs the dirty linen of Manson and Jonestown. Piecemeal borrowings of technique and style. Chants. Funny spelling.

Most of all at this particular time I need these people, though thankfully nowhere near as much as they need me.

'We are utterly serious in everything we do,' he said,

reaching for my hand across the table. Oh yes, my dear, oh yes. Before I lost his beaming face amongst the smoke that poured from my mouth: an uncontrolled, bizarre and diesel halitosis! . . . .

from February, 1983

As for my latest friend, her name is Cwissie, according to her own impediment. I am beguiled by her absolute whiteness. I visit in her crusty flat. The electricity's been cancelled, which means she'll ruin her bloody eyes. There's a battery cassette player — I bought her a recent *Cure* and some *Simple Minds* — but she's possessed by an ingenuous belief that *Beatles* music will remain "relevant" forever. She's a reformed (in the pop-group, rather than medical sense of the word) drug addict; so needless to say she sells my presents, bar the vodka. She's confided to me thirty times that she made a sigil for a "Carl" whilst coming off her heroin. She says she still might have V.D. and thinks it wiser that I never actually enter her; so we've gone "vegetarian". (I'm sorry, everything with her is in inverted commas, I'm afraid). We lie there side by side in the cat's-bowl sun of midday: soldiers on duty against the pyjama-stripes of her mattress. I masturbate her, then change hands for myself: a true Arab in that regard. She wishes she could have orgasms like mine. She has a severe depression in her breast bone which she calls her "sunken treasure chest". And of course I love her and I care for her. Enough to dry her cum-tears. Or her Beatle-tears. And to forgive the tiny volcano-shapes her cigarettes forever make in the armchair vinyl, that she calls "verches" . . . . .

'I've developed this exquisite variation,' said Terry, placing his unfaithful arm across the padded shoulder of the nearest chair.

'I chain myself naked to the inside of my front door, feet above the head, held inescapably by a padlock, the key to which I've mailed to myself an hour or so before!'

I watched the man at the adjoining table straighten;

contemplate his entree, as if it somehow were a consequence of Terry's tale.

'I've always thought that one should come from sex as one does from *An Affair to Remember:* exhausted, damp and delirious that one's limbs are still intact!'

It was a wonderful encounter, Terrence after all these years and still alive.

'I'm managing this band,' I said. 'We're concentrating on the mutilation specialists at the moment. Murderous guitars and lots of close-ups: genitalia pierced by rings. That sort of stuff.'

'Ah, heavy metal.'

'Oh really!' said the man at the next table, abandoning his garlic calamari.

'I'll shed the dreary tunesmiths by the end of the month. Want to form a band?'

He suddenly grew serious.

'Carl, I am very concerned. Don't these people jangle? I mean, walking down the street — they'd be like a kindergarten orchestra!' Then toasting his acceptance added 'One ring at a time's enough for me! Oh by the way, what's our name?'

'*Spare Parts. Spares* for short.'

'And who'll be singing lead?'. . . .

One thing: they found my dearest Winifred in her room. A window had broken during the night and the poor old thing had frozen to death.

No feathers. No claw-marks. No slimy fish. Just a face, oddly streamlined by the cold.

Carl.

from March, 1983

Dear Julia,

I have read from the books of Terrence's excess. I am hung from my feet — a cold bath-enamel screetching at my back — fat buddha, close to God. My buttocks costumed in their tartan of welts; muscles clutching at these vegetable intrusions; my testicles a drooping clothes-peg mace.

I push. I mix this trinity of liquids out of which my love shall birth. I scream for her: the sigil mark above her head — this dark sex of woman belonging so little to the world; this unnameable; this one — a beauty and an agony of thorns. O vowels! Who have called so long. . . . .

from April, 1983

from May, 1983

And whilst her lipping flutters in the brown flesh of this distant race, within the dark aquarium of fluid, they feed against you, kiss you: salmon-pout or herring-bite.

They likewise spasm, sisters: the medusa heads of teat. Their inches bloat within your mouth and shudder at the throat, ribboned with the long pale cottons of surrender.

Until pushing down the long thick waste of that desire

— bursting veil and corrugation — you are expelled; withdrawn and floundering in air, smothered with the scales of death. . . . .

And through all this no word, unless this rasping of abandon: the act of speech some rougher adze-work, and these cries its shavings, curled and grained. . . . .

Already these stupendous offers on the earlier videotapes. And now the records of performance. The heavy silver rings in their collisions. And what they must take for her breasts, these blunted areolae pyramids. And what they must take for her sweat, darkening the fabric of her clothes ...

This voyage of performance through the black ocean of dance. How she bends her head back towards them, makes a bowl for them: the sounds ridiculous. A bubbling. A porridge coming to the boil. How her face alights with crawling fluid. . . . .

I take possession of my rooms: white on white, in High Beech Road. Now my blessed hags desert me. Sustained by all these possibilities within A ———, I emanate no more desire. Nor patience with their creases, their gums and their slippers, and the ripple of their sagging, stinking flesh; their pasty batter-thick soft-centres! . . . .

from June, 1983

Terrence and I returned to High Beech yesterday to find the front door open, so we rightly expected some disaster.

Inside the dome-room, suspended side by side, like chimes, were two young girls — the tipped chairs beneath them. Perfectly still by now. Naked. White on white. We recognized them: sisters from the dreary tunesmith days. Their nipples grown exceptionally large. White on white. Absolute. . . . .

I rang Warren for a quick opinion on our legal status, say re. filming; or our obligation to report the "crime" immediately, you know. He suggested that we'd stand a reasonable chance on both, so I had *Spares* put down a bracket.

Some excellent close-ups, with a small amount of evidence gone astray. Terrytoon ended with a thorough depilation job on the thinner of the two, and some excellent tongue-work which should guarantee him an exotic disease for life!

We knew we were talking very big money here. . . .

from July, 1983

A brief fear of imprisonment. Terrytoon's case adjourned for several months. All excellent publicity. . . .

'Mr Brouwer?' the Inspector asked, as if he might possibly be mistaken, and introduced himself as Giles, as if that too might be in doubt.

He had seen the smoke coming from my mouth as he entered and nudged the ashtray on the table slightly closer, looking for the cigarette.

'Would you term yourself a libertarian, sir?'

'Taurean, actually.'

He paused.

'Yes, well where you come from it may well be fashionable to India-club one liners, but I've got two dead girls out there ...'

'By all means show them in,' I said, standing.

'They *were* members of your cult, weren't they?'

'I'm not aware of *having* a cult, Inspector. Perhaps you're thinking of "Charles" rather than "Carl's".'

And so on, until in a rare flourish of rhetoric he told me he'd "have my balls for this".

'Yes, well you look after *your* two little ones and I'll look after *mine*.'

'Look Mr Brouwer, I have every reason to believe that there has been sexual interference with a dead girl . . .'

'And,' I interrupted, 'my strictly expensive legal advice

gives *me* every reason to believe that *I* can't be charged on *your* sexual fantasies. It tells me that if two over-sexed young gels decide to get away from it all in my front room, that's not my responsibility. It's probably what they're *doing* these days. Check out *Vogue:* there's probably a photospread on it.'

As I left, I could see the shining arse of his trousers through the glass partition. He was crawling on all fours searching for my cigarette. . . . .

And then the twenty-first firm offer — "instructions from my client" and "exclusive rights of use and reproduction of" — all the endless euphemisms and figures ending graciously in five "O"s, as if already expressing their delight . . . . .

Assembling a clip from the dome-room footage, I began to understand the power of her form: there was no such thing as a single "frame"; only a shimmering instability; a metamorphosis. A crawling away of pointillism towards every vacant space. A reassembling. Each trace a multitude of other traces. A stitching of water.

She was in essence more "electronic", more "particled" than that technology could capture. And only belief. Only these camels through the needle's eye: a slow dark caravan of thread.

Carl.

from August, 1983

Dear Julia,

In a newspaper, I found an aspect of her face unknown to me. As if this new appearance were the attribute of someone else's desire. As if that city had some quarter held in secret from me. The black unchartered streets of the medina. A resistance. As if within a room, a bookcase had concealed a stairway (leading . . .) and I were merely noticing an arc of scuffing on the floorboards; a peculiar fingerprinting on the shelf-dust.

I spend the evenings staring at this photograph, straining my recollection of the drawings. Perhaps I have forgotten. I enclose the photograph. Would it be possible for you to locate it. Find her, even the smallest part. A trace amongst the drawings that I sent to you. . . . .

Then nothing. And I ending these extracts — having made of them a story, so far — and Carl, lost!

4 Sydney

Poor attempt.
Your body is no longer whole.
You feel this loss.
You fail to understand
the meaning of these extracts
or what must be done
to release their meaning.
You find incoherence where it should cohere.
You find ambiguity
where you would expect exposition.
Ellipsis
where there should be digression.
You find metamorphosis,
You find limitation and intensity,
You find contraction
in place of their more sensible opposites.
You have already sent away for books of criticism.
(They arrived, remember, in a large
white padded envelope, with stamps
to the value of over five dollars.)
And still this is another language.
Traduisez les phrases suivantes.
You feel this loss.
These luggages abandoned on
a foreign platform.
How can you reconstruct this history?
Poor work.

I had awoken, screaming at my loss — an expectation of my neck a mass of blood desire. I bolted from the bed, holding my fingers to my eyes.

Everywhere I felt her trace within this room. The

skid-marks of a jewellery across the skin, drizzled in a sex-exhaustion.

Everywhere an evidence of recent disappearances: a cushion pile, still warm; a book marked at the passage about "falling"; grey nipples of ash. The rings of coffee-cups on table-tops. On the pillow-white, the watermark of gasping mouths: faintness of blood or lip shiraz.

Wondering if I should perhaps have signed myself as Julia — who had become her now, so much, in this; and knowing that we must shortly meet again, ourselves, if not before this last reply — I wrote to Aosman.

But then, perhaps I had already learned enough.

A fashion spread from *Triste*.

The pale mouths, perfect. The contrasts electric. The look of the blurred eye: no hard lines. Eyelids misted; veiled in colour.

Thirty-six exposures. Motor driven camera. Proof-sheet printed intact. And yet this one and several woman: how could she ever be these endless sisters and the same?

Enough. I knew her instantly. And those desires I kept from you before — so blunt, so brutal and disgusting — that *need* to ————————————————————
————————————————————————————————————
———————— so indefensible in a writing such as this, I knew was equally a part of her. And I began to understand how only that woman who has been summoned by desire — and thus a consequence of it — can hope to cure this unbearable want: that everything around you give you its utter attention. Think only of you. Care only for you.

Have you heard the one about the two fanettes last seen swinging on the grapevine? Plus rumours that a certain un-named group may just have launched a new craze of snuff-rock videos! But we'll Spare you the details.

July, 1983

Then there is the by now notorious (by invitation) stage act, if you've managed to catch it — and Lilly Law obviously hasn't as yet — during which, amongst other peasant delights, our lead singer refreshes herself courtesy of any number of willing male fans, and pops through the finale, her face gleaming with appreciation. All good clean fun I'm sure, but hardly good for the diet! Then how come I'm all ears, and, more importantly, Uncle Sam to the tune of some hundred-thousands worth? Intrigued? Then stay tuned. Plus if you hear of any Spare tickets going . . .

September, 1983

The chic and vapid journalese of rock. But Carl?

May, 1984

Dear Mr Aosman,

I write again seeking any information you may have concerning the whereabouts of Carl Brouwer, a guest I believe at your house between June and November, 1982 . . .

And then that letter, ten weeks distant; and that appalling fact. Arriving as if part of our first winter: not in Aosman's hand, but Zora's; having misread my name for "Walton".

I thank you for your letter, but no first letter arrived at this house. I trust you understand.

Mr Aosman cannot himself reply to your letter having suffered *une attaque* since three months. He can no longer write, nor speak, and much of what you ask must now remain with him, and unknown. I have however copied the sigil formula and include a copy of it with this letter.

Carl returned to Fès towards the end of 1983, probably October, and left shortly before the end of the year. I believe he was intending to return to Sydney, Australia.

The final weeks here were not happy times. I remember much of it as being spent in silence and solitude: unthinkable in this place!

Carl was a man beset with jealousies. He detested most of all the happiness of others, as if he believed joy to be a finite quantity: everything must diminish *him.* In every beginning he saw an end. But it is not my place to cast shadow on lives already sufficiently dark.

I have passed on the formality of your regards to Mr Aosman.

'Yes, I saw him,' said Julia.

I remember her, white bedclothes, sitting up. Her thighs covered by the roses quilt — the squares in their alternation with the zodiac — and she, covering her face with her hands: loss.

The Venetian blinds opened onto darkness; slats like horizontal swords.

'He was here in this room. A week before I gave you the

letters. Oh Christ, Finch, I'm sorry. It's just if you'd have seen him . . .'

She stopped. What remained of pride or strength within her posture giving way completely, like some paper crumpled in the hand: a gesture of an absolute defeat.

'They're in the drawer.' And she pointed to the furthest corner of the room, as if I were a child disgraced, in need of punishment.

I wondered what she might have seen, but never said, that could have first occasioned this elaborate lie. Whether it had been a genuine attempt to obfuscate the truth: to have me, as I might have almost done, approach her with that sensible admission "I simply do not know", and live within the memory of that "truth".

Or had she known. Rehearsed a thousand times the miseries of this evening. That only through a lie would she be forced into a meeting with the unbearable. What fearsome vision, these bizarre ventriloquies; I simply do not know.

I took them from their bright surrounds of past — the postcards and mementoes — their weight gunheavy, the four remaining letters, bound like some perversion, and I held them in my grasp: these four months of absence and this end.

Another day had passed: the envelopes before me, with the dreadful burden of their substance, still untouched.

Perhaps now, I thought, she will be free of him — until I saw how she could never be free, irrespective of the answer; who could never bear that final word to live with — who loved him, who loved him, who loved him. And that desire I felt quite suddenly for her, so bound.

But why do I bother confessing this to you, or even to myself? Who wanted everything; the taste of every woman — whom I wanted — until I could no longer want.

I am not so different from him for whom she grieves, I thought. As you are from me, I expect.

And after all, had not the very first of English novels developed from the letter?

Aosman's Formula

1

Prepare the sigil, the name-shape of this most desired, this her.

2

Forget, except in moments when your body is convulsed by an extreme.

3

Exhaust the body through your breath and posture. Rehearse the stillest dance.

4

Obtain the urn. That death-mask of the penis thoroughly engorged.

5

Ejaculate her name, precisely as you spill inside the urn.

6

Seal the urn with the sigil mark.

7

At midnight and the moon a quartered blade, a cuticle and of your hand, bury the urn.

8

At the waning moon, retrieve the urn and pour the contents as libation into earth. Replenish as is necessary with a newly-brought familiar. Sing her name these final times, and close the open cask of earth, the urn within.

That night I had awoken to apparent storm. The room adrift to shrill and dissipated thunder; a turbulence, fire and flock-centred: the ninety angels, trapped within the outline of this *Aerial Vampire*; a bizarre, contorted fleshing paper.

'Reunite with us,' they whispered, this profusion of luxuriant imaginings. 'We are all otherness which is your past.'

These incarnations calling urgently to me.

'Realize all otherness as self,' they crooned, the myriad lids rustling before me to display. The feathered inks of areolae that spread their darknesses across the breast.

I snapped the cigarette lighter into flame.

Their screaming filled the room. Acridity of burning feathers. Burning paper. Shadowmass that shuffled to these letters. A stillness. A faint residual crackling of air. They reassembled to the substances of charcoal, ink, of pastel and wash.

'One day I found a collection of pornography,' Julia had said, how many years before. 'Photographs of his. One of the women had her mouth. One her hair. Another I suppose his idea of her cunt . . .'

This history so "irrevocably determined" as he obviously knew himself; borne away in waves and lost in darkness and distance.

And what of that other photograph he had sent of A——— . That aspect of her face unknown to him. That trace he craved amongst the angel-drawings he had sent to Julia.

I rummaged through the letters for that August and its foul betrayals. I held the lighter to the photograph, clipped from a daily newspaper; the face unflinching from the heat-light; the myriad dots quite powerless and fixed. There was no movement. I stared at these unknown features — not her, nor him — his obsession leaking, spilling across every face, slowly running from him.

The photograph of a stranger. A simple unknown man in this precise dimension of his terror.

5 London / Fès

from September, 1983

At this pinnacle I falter. Her voice calls to me, broken into knives of frequencies. Her bodies open in their focusses; then snap together like a bamboo fan.

Only yesterday she gave the answer to a question I had never asked — nor thought of asking. . . . .

Who am I to her? How can I hope to bring her to these thousand orgasms? Learn for each of her what satisfies? In absence I can feel her every movement; through rooms like the passage of air on summer evenings. Her voices talking to another: intimate and open and subdued, as they might have once to me, who can no longer satisfy. . . . .

Abattis of nail. The twenty moons break free of the hand. Their whiteness burns. The tides engulf. Examine the coin's face: everything bears these marks. There is the same order in the indentations of fingernails in book-covers. A savage scything. Half-moons of desire. . . . .

Perhaps she grows ill. Her sweat an acid: the act of love elaborate etching. I feel her nails bite deep into my flesh. Even as I enter her I feel the hairs grow; the breasts slide down beneath my chest. I reel from the stench of her genitals.

Perhaps she is rotting outwards from her sex. . . . .

Last night returning from a cray at Terrences, I met the dogs emerging from the violet half-moon shadows; breaking from the stone. They failed to recognize me and I ran in fear from my own house. They would savage me, having also smelt my terror.

I must return to Aosman. I shall place Terrytoon in

charge of our finances — a ridiculous move — but so much the better. It will, I believe, make it easier for all of us.

Carl.

from October, 1983

Dear Julia,

Mid Autumn and still this sun. I drove immediately to the South to stare out at that brutality of the Atlas and the desert beyond. Vainglories, powers, dust. The grain of landscape: desert and face, disturbed, ephemeral.

It was as if I had set out those forty days to Tomboctu: an insane army to conquer a careless citadel. The city is a desert. It absorbs us. It marries us into its families, into its line. And so defeats us. . . . .

Aosman has aged. At first we sat in silence, the columning of ash the room's only movement. He sat erect in his Hoffman chair with a regard of mild disdain. Then he arose to play the four last songs. Richard Strauss. Nick Drake. Sublime or ridiculous you might say, but there was a sense of everything being equalled.

He looked up at me, breathing smoke.

'And what you set out to achieve, you have achieved, yes?'

'Yes.'

'Against incredible odds, I suppose.'

'Yes.'

'These daring ideas have been vindicated? The power of the imagination has triumphed? Acclaim? Approval?'

'Yes.'

'A certain sand-pit enjoyment, would you say?'

I looked up at him. The ring appeared to have melted into his finger and he, still breathing out that pencil-line of smoke. . . . .

Zora moves through these rooms as if in answer to a wailing child. Light falls upon her, constantly divided, making of her a zebra likeness. At night, as consequence, the unease of zebras.

I believe all attempts to domesticate this animal have failed. . . . .

Last week I walked to the café seeking the love of the child Ginette. Her girl-face frightened me. Her hands reached up to touch my beard (of neglect), then made a mocking circle about her lips. Beard of hands.

'Regardes-moi!' she cried. 'Je porte une barbe aussi!' And showed me the recent sparse hairs of her mound.

'You grow old,' I said.

But I was frightened of these whore's eyes, glinting from the body of this twelve-year-old; knowing her powers clearly could exceed my own.

I could not help but take her, somewhat roughly, as if to bite the energy from her. The mound-bone and the hipbones and the scouring ribs wounded me long after: as if I had been severely beaten by sticks. . . . .

And so she led me to her sister. The begging process in its inevitable multiplication.

We entered the dark, fetid confines of this single room in which maybe seven people slept and ate and bred. Against the back wall, as if breaking from a relief, perhaps it was her twin, who stood swaying in the airless shadow of this place. Meeting my eyes. Who had obviously been born without arms. . . . .

from November, 1983

These aberrations. Was it not the hairs: too thick or dark, too numerous — fountaining from the mole; stroked upon the upper lip; single coarse hairs that fell leaf-like from the cunt across the inner thigh; areolae hair, in oasis — and this, for example, alone which made your intolerable beauty bearable?

And would it not be an ecstasy then to stare at these genitals knowing the nose to be broken, the leg withered, the feet malformed, the palate cleft . . .

That even as I worked on A ———, towards that variant perfection, I always wanted her, how shall I say it — "incomplete". And when at first I gazed upon the bodies of our hanging sisters . . .

The rigor of death is so absolute and generous. Those evenings when we had our sisters drink liqueurs of sperm. Their beauty revolted us. How it managed to survive their baldness, the tattoos. It survived their mouths held open for our defaecation; it survived their gagging and their vomiting; it survived the enemas and starvation. It survived the bastinado and the dislocation of their bones.

But not our love. . . . .

The temple has written to me here. I have thoroughly examined their letters for numbers. Perhaps the secret time of my release.

They say that A ——— has become pregnant by an animal. It is impossible. But I also know that it will come to pass. This judgment. That she will die of the weight and size within her: gleaming in stupendous pain. That they will be concerned to capture all these moments on tape. . . . .

from December, 1983

It is finished. Perhaps I am frightened of these last excesses. This paper wall between myself and numbness. Do you understand how I might have everything. How possible this absolute might be. And how important it is that I be prevented from this possibility. . . . .

A fortnight ago I slept with Zora. Not a word was spoken: perhaps we shared the same spite. It satisfied my curiosity, if at an extravagantly inflated price. I cared so little I maintained a most tolerable erection. . . . .

Aosman rarely comes from his room, or does so with incredible stealth. I feel like a child punished by his parents' inattention. Every day I wonder if perhaps he might not have died in there. I listen for the faintest trace of movement, as a woman might dwell upon the sleeping body of her lover, seeking presence of breath.

This house has become a prison in which each seeks to display a finer suffering. . . . .

Last week I knocked on Zora's door, opening it without waiting for acknowledgement. She was masturbating. She stared at me with neither desire nor embarrassment.

'I am dead' she said. 'I am past it. I cannot even interest myself.'

'I know,' I replied. . . . .

There was a razor-flint shriek. A lightning glare, brief and sickening. A blackness. And all desires flowed slowly from me — waking to the strong bromides of air. A ghastly defloration darkening the bed. I have summoned a local healer: no European will see this.

An un-sexed figure approaches me across the sands of this room. The goddess-crazed Attis, transforming in his misery. The still-point of the turning world. Still dance. The hot still air of film.

And how far is this dance from that of the young Art student? How far is this from the dance of Matisse? How far from the writhing mass in the concerts? How far from the two sisters bobbing like marionettes?

How far from Zora and Aosman's foxtrot? . . . .

I am returning. It is finished. You have listened to my history — seen how irrevocably it is determined. I leave tomorrow, unburdened.

Your silence above all else has exhausted me. It is as much a lie as my confession. Do not be proud therefore of your abstinence — your cardinal sin of omission — my bloated and precious priest. My love. My downfall. What might we say knowing this, any of this were public?

Perhaps everything. Perhaps everything, when the time comes.

Carl.

6 Sydney

The morning I first came inside Julia, we would remain until the end of August together. She announced this fact with an appalling sadness — I failed to understand the necessity for such a sudden ultimatum — then refused to say any more of it. She slept, or feigned sleep; then waking (or . . .) spoke briefly of a need now to be quiet.

That Friday, earliest August, and some sixteen days before, I had come to her for what I thought a final visit — knowing there was nothing left to be rehearsed, no special way of saying: just that single word.

The previous week the air had constant thunder stillness; sudden total light; a humidity of stale clothes. She agreed to a night of sex, openly, and without hesitation.

Her reaction to foreplay had been so intense I could not bring myself to interrupt it by entering her. I later learned to look upon these occasions as "gifts" in that she never sought to touch me. When it was over for her . . .

She lit a single soft-pack cigarette; held it from her like a long-stemmed glass.

'It's just that when you ask me how I feel, as soon as I start to talk about it, all the feeling goes. You're a writer, why don't you simply make me up.'

I often thought her one mistake was having made this trespass in my life — and mine, having mistaken it for love, or the possibility of love.

But then again, I think I can remember her remarking on

an earlier occasion that the orgasm should most properly conclude in tears.

'I'm sorry.' And she crushed her cigarette into the matchbox lid. The still air briefly tainted with that memory of burning angels.

I wondered how I could have lost her then, or held her; already having made this possible, impossible. Then rain.

I moved quietly from the bed and drew aside the curtains, compelled as always to watch the falling. Selah.

'Finch,' she said; I heard her say. 'When you write about all this — how much is going to be true?'

Curved and indivisible,
the daylight cannot catch her, falling
deep within this arabic of stance.
Cannot hold her, breaking through
the hands of afternoon.

That Sunday, when she spoke of what
she could not promise; as her body
furthered to the merest brooch of dusk.
A problem of uncertainty
against the certain sky.

And only she can stop it, only
crying 'Stop!' (But how delicious
all this learning how to fall). And what
half-finished argument, what fraction
of those sentences,

what other sense to be construed
— who falls asleep between your very words —
is carried with her, out of reach,
. . . falling, turning in her numeral sleep,
away from me.

What compensates for everything we have seen?
Who forgives us everything we know?
Now that we had all betrayed, and been betrayed.

'It's just . . .' she said, and then fell silent. Perhaps I should have made a sentence of it, completed it, as now eventually I have. But then, perhaps it was complete.

'That night, I can remember waking, thinking that the room was underwater and gasping for air and almost choking on its presence.

He was standing just in front of me — he'd been watching me, I think — white, bloated, speaking softly to me; swaying in the darkness like some ghastly begging fish.

Finch, I can't forget the way he looked . . .'

But by then I had already seen him.

Catullus 63

Below him there was darkness gathering.
Attis come to Phrygia, to yew-woods
and to wreaths, to shrouds of this dark centre.

First the sea. Then as he ran, the shadow
draining from him until darker moons
of heat were spat on dust, and padded feet
that fell to earth. But always darknesses.
Still within his palm, the flint whose razor-
edge had slashed his balls' weight from the groin.
Unburdened, now she understood the pain
of this *menarche.* These whitened fingers seeking
the redemption of her drum from earth;
the sacred drum of sacrifice, Cybele!
Shaking at the empty bull-skin; trembling,
chanting to her gathering familiars:
'Go there! You, my likenesses, my exiles,
ever searching for this other place.
Who following have made my journey's semblance,
burnt with the erosion of this rapid
salt-edged wind; your bodies equally
unmanned through excess of this loving-hate.
You, who cannot stand here, rid yourselves
amongst this forest; let the swiftness of
your movement please her. Go there, to Cybele!
Where the shelling cymbal-voices clash;
the shuddering-hollow drums resound. To where
the flautist deeply mouths the curving reed;
and Maenads fling their raw and moistened heads,
mane-wreathed in ivy. Where the restless, shaking
goddess-pack habitually career.
To find this other place! Let us be gone!'
So the tribe of ecstasy in screetch-chords,
every eel-tongue bloated, flicking out
in seizures of imagination; every
drum-skin bellow answered by the cymbal,
coiled towards the darkening Ida-green.
Before them, Attis clamoured senseless through
the thickening growth: a heifer still unbroken,
rasping, lung-burnt, chafing at the burden
of the yoke; the rush of Gallae drum beat
frenzied and stampeding at her trace.
At last within the goddess-woods, the wasted
pack fell in exhaustion — food beyond them,
starved of sleep — their eyes were overwhelmed;

their rabid furor lidding into night.
Attis woke to sun-snort. Rustling. Brittle-
timber torched by eyes. Until horizons
reared and broke: a white horse sped across
the corrugated sea to earth, and trampled
every shadow underneath its hooves.
Sleep deserted Attis for the brided
arms of Pasithea. And so, abandoned
to the furor-memory of loss,
in anguish she retraced that shoreward path;
where, looking to the sea's peripheral
immensity — veiled behind the onset
of these woman-tears — she cried in grief
as any mourner, leaning to her home:
'And have I left you, City bearing me,
and City of my birth: a slave escaping
domination for these dominating
woods of Ida; to be lost forever
in the frozen cunt-lairs of the savage;
to approach that hidden wilderness?
Where are you — eyes that want you mine — now I
may speak outside that brief parenthesis
of ecstasy? And have I lost you: forum,
wrestling school, gymnasium; the taste
of cinders, burning here, from hearth and track.
And have I lost you, poor and poor, again
this heart's wild turn of grief. What form has not
been mine: this Attis, woman, man; this Attis,
youth or boy. My body oiled and massive
ever hard between you, cradle-locked
in arguments of flesh. My doorway crowded;
threshold warmed with visitors. And there!
The sun itself has led me, Attis, from
the bedroom under canopies of flowers ...
By what name shall I now be known? As *she,*
the goddess-slave, the handmaid of Cybele?
Maenad, half-himself, the "I" of penis
ever lost? And shall I now abide
forever in these forest slopes of Ida,
smothered in the whitenesses of snow
and ice; beneath these flinted peaks, forever

forested alone with wandering boar,
or wooded with the deer. Beloved City,
who will ever hear me now? And now
this deep regret. And now and now, this shame.'
Cybele listened to these words that flowed
between her red-stained lips. The chariot lions
having fallen silent, stirring — nostrils
spreading — searching for the stringent prey-blood
of her speech. And so the goddess, freeing
the lion (left, flock-tearing lion) cried:
'Relentless one, infuriate him! Stalk him
into madness! He who so desires
his freedom shall remain within my woods
eternally possessed. Now go! Your back
perpetually wounded by the lashing tail.
Endure this pain that every place might thunder
to your raging bellow. Let your mane
bleed rivers through the muscles of the neck!'
Self-goading into fury now, the beast slashed
blade to blade, until the vegetation
bled and whitened, foam-flecked, at its passage.
On the dampened shore-sand, lined by white,
girl-Attis stood against the marbled waves.
She heard the tide-wash ruptured once again
by padding feet — the lion broke towards her
out across the sand — and ran in terror
to the forest; to the wild enslaving
darkness spilling ever from the wound.

O Cybele, goddess of the Mount,
keep this madness distant from my house!
Possess *other* men! Make *others* mad!

Carl Brouwer, December 1981

❖❖❖

Entering the cold of that apartment was like being underwater. Standing in the doorway, looking down the corridor; and from the front room where I could just discern the furthest edge of a man, dressed identically to myself, standing by the entrance. These were the geometries I had expected: arriving as I saw myself arrive. And these animations: as from time to time the doors trapped shut; the window-frames dropped bladed like a guillotine.

I walked along these whitened corridors. In the bathroom hung *Le Pendu,* fat buddha, close to God, exposed amongst his ordure. On the balcony outside the rooms, her white dress rose-smothered, *L'Impératrice* reclined upon a cushioned couch; star-rise, star-set in her crown of black. Just as, and only at that strict appointed time, the twenty cuticles shall break free from the hand, and, in the street below, Carl, returning from his cray at Terrences, shall run in fear from the harrowing dogs beneath *La Lune sauvage.*

And everywhere these traces could be found; these twenty-two black stations of the cross.

He was frozen, bloated like the old de Sade, on the wooden boards of this floor; having used the carpet as a blanket. The dust around his body was quietly reassembling, fleshing, with the purposefulness of ants.

I pulled aside the covering. Surely this city is a desert, that might claim his sex as reward for these secrets. Primitively attained: a hacking. The age of the wounds suggested Morocco, but as to whose hand had occasioned this — or why? But I have no medical training. I presume though, it was in this state that he exposed himself to Julia.

Carl dead? I failed to comprehend it. Did not believe. Would not accept. This man suspended from the scaffold of the sigil. This unnecessary theatre.

I searched these rooms, how long, more thoroughly, for

something which might explain. Might have shed this pale and wallowed form.

When do we concede? At what overwhelming point of knowledge? And if so, why not now?

The English novel is not unlike him: a friend grown old, anachronistic; gone in search of some impossible truth; full of style. An individual with a marked sense of tradition, who over time becomes corrupt, obese and self-destructive; who we continue (quite despite ourselves) to love. Even to this present point.

Each night I take this man to bed within my solitary sleep. Make love to him, and hold him to my sexuality of self.

I remember how it is the sheer enormity of men when close: the hair of their bodies; the chisel-edge of stubble. The abrasion that encloses every kiss. All love with men is of necessity submission. I understand how they might be hated for their breath, their sweat, their size . . . or might be loved.

And what is left to understand of Carl — (look to see if now perhaps the foreskin has been pierced) his balls, contracted walnut-tight beneath my touch; his penis like a forearm tightly held against the sweating belly.

Moving, scratching out this perfect biography, I can no longer keep these characters from myself. As it is no longer possible to tell exactly who is involved in our love-making.

By dawn I still had found no sleep. I heard these scuttlings from below, and women's voices carried by the pipes: half-flute, half-chime.

I heard the sound of cutlery, clutched and regimented against silver trays. I heard the trill of hurried footsteps, stride-checked by their uniforms. For some this day had also just begun; as another day had passed.

I sat before the window, looking out across the rooftops: this cathedral mossing slate. The chair gasped, swallowed air against the boards.

I began to move these letters, massaging them into the table-top in swirling motion; the divination of a lover to his lover's body. I began to write, as always with the terror of beginning.

And perhaps, in one sense, it would have been far easier for all of us, for me to simply say to you as I had simply turned to Julia, saying: "No."

F.W.
August/September, 1984

ST CLAIR

If I has become another, the poet's only chance of embodying it is from the moment he starts to become himself again; he is given the possibility of expressing what goes beyond him when he too is reborn as an obstacle. That is the paradox and the basic contradiction of poetic activity.

André Frénaud

1 An Opening Description

A persistence of winter. Grey storm clouds
of smoke from the mills beyond St Clair
dredge beneath a half-risen moon. Enough smoke
to net the late-returning flock of birds.
Ghosted in a laboratory coat, Warren steadied
himself at the kitchen steps, looking out beyond
the courtyard: its brickwork sweating overflow,
steam exhaling from pipe-ends. *Another trial.*
This journey constantly retaken. The exhausting
necessity of possession. Another beginning,
how is it possible? Warren moved out amongst
the drums, their dull ballistic columns spent
on cobble, along the masonry of the lane.
The constant superstitious hand prodding out
a loosened brick. Cigarettes. A kitchen staff
paying for what, he thought. And what of him?
Of you, my brother. What were your thoughts
on the mud-shod journey to truth? When you came,
drugged, into these last turrets of nationalism.
The soot-devil sewn across the countryside
into furrows, into the cracks of the skin,
into rows of the football mass and the lungs
of the miners' choir. *Do you understand?*
Do things seem clearer now? Knowing these
questions, their sulphazin, and their faint
trace of turpentine?

2 In Which The Last of The Legitimate Patients Considers His Health

I am little better. And hardly well.
'This morning I failed to clear the fence.
Felt my hands give to cold soil. The bother
of washing. Clothes, elbows, thoroughly wetted.
No injury, but the humiliation.' Finchley
closed an earlier Tuesday. Suddenly we are
re-born old.
A child runs out on the field,
conscious of the whiteness of his legs,
tugging the socks above his knees. He hovers
on the perimeter of action, dodging, braking,
flailing the arms when running — "girlish" —
he has heard. The ball curves back at him.
But the cold-block hands, frozen by wind into
a mitten of flesh, cannot stretch around
the ball, only register sting. No injury,
but the humiliation. Memory of cold leather.
A phlegm: not fear, but the corruption of doubt
always within us.
Suddenly we are re-born old,
and spend the rest of our lives acting against
this solemn truth. Perhaps a dozen times
we hear something approximate a scream: wounds
too slow to heal; chest pain; the failures of
relationship. From where he sat, Finchley
could see a margin of lawns linking St Clair
to the old summer guest house. Lawns the size
of playing fields, dormant for winter recess.
An only child his parents had brought with
scarecrow purpose into the fields of love.
And like a child knowing, in illness as in
threat, that what must be done is to keep
perfectly still.

3 A View from A Train

Merry's letter marked a passage
from Michaux concerning trains. In this he
imagines wax or clay sculptures set regularly
beside the track, each a fine gradation of
gesture which when passed at a certain speed
would burst into motion. Sheehan passed
a dotard-line of valley housing, herded
against the track. Scarved and netted women
waiting at their steps, looking out toward
the mill for the trudging lines of *Afternoon.*
The carriage door shot back. An involuntary
gasp for air — a snorer woken by his noise —
and all submerged beneath a fury of grey suits.
A sickened wish, too late, that he'd said less.
But where? The details gone. A speech. Petition.
The squeak of natural justice. The sudden fear
he'd wet himself — but no way now to check.
He wanted most to cry for her, so far. The letter
that was left of her. And now it was inevitable:
not fear, but dreadful sadness. Deep regret.
Sheehan remembered the first three blows for
what they brought him up against: reflection
of a carriage window, the grease-smear of
his own forehead; the heavy brocade of a "first-
class" seat, smelling of dust and arses; floor.
An unsmoked cigarette beneath the seat.
Nothing else.

Halted at the junction for
the through-train, Murray watched the glinting
maze of rails. Bitter morning. Scaffolds up-ended.
Sheehan propped like a drunkard in the corner
with his luggage and his map of Ecuador.

4 The Homunculus Child

The homunculus child
might understand his nakedness as punishment
before the mirror. Might bring a riddled piebald
flesh from fire, the prickle scorching of the spine
and tuck his sex for an improper *mons Veneris,*
covering up the paltry flatness of his chest
with shame.
What made us turn with such vengeance
to ourselves? A life in this exhausting pursuit.
The punishment we need against the fear of pain.
Continue this work, explain ourselves, and
never make amends?
The moon was higher now,
whiter than before. He watched the whiter fingers
of mill smoke merge to a fist, and the arm, into
the torso of Satan. Warren would burn his coat.
Watch it ignite with the months of turpentine.
Rid himself of the smell, and with it burn away
the questions.

5 A Shorter History of The Insane

At evening, pigeons gather
on stone ledges of the East, as if Finchley
had drawn to his neck an extravagant lace.
From the lane Warren saw him, frozen in his
neurotic stance — the last visible posture
of respectability — as if wealth itself had
dispossessed him of all physical prowess.

On a day unsuitably embalmed in sunlight,
and eighteen months ago, the government
acquired St Clair: home, hotel, a hundred years
of insanities (both seasonal and permanent);
the lawns and their pavilion. And having missed
the summer trade, they opened to a new insane.
Opened their skins to turpentine, and their
veins to purified sulphur. *Has this helped you?*
Are you beginning to understand?

Warren
felt drugged by the massed cooing. An endless
refolding of spoons. These artichokes.
This plump-beaded abacus of dusk. Finchley
still at the window of his first-floor room:
the legitimate face of convalescence at bay
in the disused East. Their eyes met. It might
as well have been an aeroplane, Warren thought,
for all his looking out. That longing for
an inaccessible world.

6 Reverie

For her a kite's appropriate enough
to go unwinding in the breeze:
an offered rose upon a single stem,
a postage stamp upon the sky.
For she has learnt from older men across
the common of her pilgrimage
a clue; a tugging at the figure-eights
of art and their infinities.
A terror of the commonplace that knows
the vast importance of the line.

7 The Increasing Difficulty of Silence

As Warren leant back into the border hedge,
as the sun moved below tree-line, a figure
halted, turned — black slant of hair dividing
her back — and removed the cigarettes. No system
can eradicate these unholy orders of greed.
The dishonour and disrespect of the free.

Dear M ———,
last night I woke in the absence
of air. Mouth, nostrils, drowned in bile.
Eyes in flame. I coughed out a straw hole,
slowly sucked in breath, wiser than my body's
wish to gasp. The acid burning my throat.
The consequences of speech, and of silence.
The consequences of my name, and this sentence.
My love, they are burning my voice away.
S.

Warren's urine weaved about the cigarette butts
in the staff trough. Shoulder blades of mosaic
enamel: this arena of manhood. This high-point
of English art. And how much would a piss cost
the lunatics in bribes? He smelt the turpentine.
His hand upon wet brick. Cigarettes sliding
into a dark wall, a needle sliding into the arm:
these tamperings with the natural world. He smelt
the antiseptic blocks. He smelt his penis.
And the medication. Saw the white frames; heard
the springs of iron beds tear like ligaments.
Sheehan. That name, and perpetual fire.

8 Reverie

I Dreamt a Dream! what can it mean?
Blake, *The Angel*

She enters me, not only
with her cunt-wet hand,
but with her nipples, swollen
thumb-thick, pushed inside
the foreskin of my cock.

And not enough, she takes me
shuddering to her mouth.
And not enough, her words
break surface, warbling through
the thickness at her lips.

'Piss on me!' she cries.
I spray. Her face is varnished,
and the pillow darkens
like a dye unfastening
from the blackness of her hair.

Warren switched on the light.
Cupping the penis with his other hand he hobbled
to the sink. He stared at his sweat-streaked face.
'Suck me!' he said. 'Suck my cunt!'
His mouth
closed upon the vagina. But her lips pursed
and clenched like a kiss, and an alien tongue
pushed in his mouth. He spat it to the sink:
a wad, the pulp of cigarettes from the urinal.
His mouth's frightful miscarriage swirling

apart in the running water. Warren looked up,
the pattern of his face dislodged by tears:
'I love you!' he said.

9 In Which a Patient Is Cured of Insanity and a Rainbow Appears

Trepping's jaundiced face bobbed. Rocked
like a small hire boat, disused in the mottled
rain-light of afternoon. 'Do you understand?'
asked Warren. If you up-end this man, is there
a keel upon his spine, and planks? Is there tar?
Or simply months of ulceration.

From the East,
the tree-tops slightly bowed, Warren looked out
towards the Mayflower Hotel. A rainbow appeared.
An antique from that earlier century. Florid
and misplaced. Exhausted by a hundred years
of rhetoric. Warren burst into a laughter
that sliced through the air like cheese-wire.
When there is nothing left to ask? 'The Flood!'
he said. Rather the flood.

Finchley sat up,
his hand moving instinctively to the light.
A bedside table. A small cabinet of books:
yellowed paper, binding brittle as fingernail.
On his mantlepiece the belligerent "shillings" of
private income. A Parthenon of silver for the gas.
'The terror of the commonplace!' he thought.

10 A Letter

My Dear M ——— ,

in one sense

you must surrender as much to relief as pain.
I have written this letter home a thousand times.
These things I cannot say, that may, may not
be published depending on my friends. Or those
of you who are not my friends. Truth is finally
a speech of the possessed, exiled by the sane
to lies, disorder or to silence.

At dawn

the ward lights flare. I have seen it before,
this "cleansing of thoughts", but never wholly beyond
the gauze of chemicals. My brother, strapped upon
his bed now for three days; spoon-fed on porridge
like an infant; no offer of bed pans. For two days
stinking in his own body waste.

I am not well.

I realize now how long this might take.
The more familiar the journey, the more
dangerous to complete. The closer this end,
the greater risk of incompletion. Another
beginning, how is it possible?

S.

11 In Which Warren Confides in Sheehan

'. . . by then he couldn't hear.
Trepping was an end for me. Rocking at the bed.
As if I'd given the injection to an animal.
I remember holding his face, his hippopotamus face,
that yellowed face in my arms. It's no surprise
for them to say "Yes, I *was* ill!" These endless
betrayals of profession, esteem. These forced
denials of a lifetime's belief. All of us!
Do you understand this country anymore?' Warren
shifted in his seat. 'And if I come to believe
in *your* truth, in your *insanity*, what exactly
do I say? What offer can I possibly make, knowing
how I'm part of this? If only the dangerous gift
of my silence, so somehow we may speak.'

12 In Which There Is A Disturbance in Finchley's Room

Finchley hadn't slept. Threat is
a chameleon of the brain that has power to change
shape and sense. Once it was the dark itself,
or things that grew from dark to live. The malady
of arrivals. A loom and squeal of obligation.
The young pigs of surprise. Awake! The sound
of single vehicles smeared over early morning.
Finchley watched his furniture inching further
from the door. A wardrobe leave its paper wad.
Abrupter coughs of chair and bedside table.
Maraca pill-jars. Somersault of pens. Walls
bulge from the corridor exploding paint-scales
in a brittle mothish storm.
The room grew still.
Finchley heard a distant scream. A scuttle
of approach. His eyes traced out the door.
A pale illumination. A phosphorescent gas.
He collapsed upon the bed, his dressing-gown
hooked with splinters, his glasses barred
with sweat. An accumulated paintwork wedged
beneath his fingernails.

13 On Truth

Are you listening to these words?
Can you ascertain their truth? For instance let me
describe the mill-smoke that squanders its cloud
across St Clair. Things I am allowed to say —
to perpetuate these tableaux of a natural world.
And if I talk of a persistence of winter, grey
storm clouds that dredge beneath a half-risen moon,
is this no longer true? So unspeakable? Or if
I tell you of the crowded lavatories. How people
search for cigarette stubs among the used paper.
How some of the patients eat their own excrement.
I don't want to blacken the picture — this did
not happen everyday. And if you find that this
is true, has this helped you? Do you feel better?

What is my belief if it willingly encompasses
a speech infected by guilt and the desire for
punishment? I am tired of truth, and its thank-
lessness. Why are these nets strung across the
open landings? Why is this cell called a "slit"?
Why is the anus of this man bleeding? Why has
this strait-jacket been soaked in water?

14 Inside Two Bedrooms

In the bedroom this same bed,
its covers drawn back in hunched retreat.
White rings contoured on an undersheet;
the washing basket's melee of straps.
It worried her, the dirt. The inevitability
of decay. She saw it in the scale upon
the pillowcase; dandruff on a lover's coat.
This same danger that attracts us, that
excites us. Would I lie to you? Warren
worked through the wardrobe, a trochaic
push of clothes across the metal bar:
ticking, blessing, recognizing nothing
of the fashion on its hangers, lining up
with its shockingly poor posture.

'I don't care what you want. Get out!'
She'd recognized the car. Had rallied
a deafness in the driveway and the hall.
Warren commandeered the disc-player,
enunciating beneath a mask of Brahms:
'There's an academic at Clair. Sheehan.
I've stopped medication.' 'So?'

Finchley
removed his suitcase from above the wardrobe.
Too heavy. Too packed with ribboned letters.
The past. The naked sterile child that
shrieked to him from corridors: beckoning.
Pale. The face of Warren staring upwards
at his window in the bars of dying light.
The pale face slowly breeding in the silver
of his mirror. It was almost five before
Finchley finished packing. He was going home.

15 In Which Warren's Ex-wife Might Be Seen to Extend The Metaphor

'. . . Because *you* say it.
Because you can't escape the things you are.
Not him, not me.' She lit a cigarette.
'Appropriation isn't change.' Blowing out
the match. 'Once upon a time it was England,
a marriage, or once maybe love. *This* time
you stop medication. Because every now and then
it's what you've got to put on the scales
to balance things out. But the other side is
still there — I know you think it isn't —
but it simply doesn't go away.' She stubbed
the cigarette. 'For Christ's sake, Carl,
how can you possibly begin to understand
what I might, what any of us might feel, be.
If you *died* for what you've told me today,
it'd simply be the same animal preening
itself; chewing off a fingernail or wiping
its fucking arse.' 'I'm sorry,' he said.
Her spittle hit his face at the corner of
the mouth. 'Would you like to piss on me?'
she asked.
Are we to be condemned by histories
in which we took no part: unable to talk of
ourselves unless it be a justification; unable
to talk of others unless we appropriate their
voice; unable to talk of this relationship
between us, unless it be from privilege?
Is *this* the only truth of speech: not what
is said, but the saying?
Mercy of the freeway
open tonight. Forgive her these words. This
dark rushing macadam. This South. These
breaches of decorum.

16 In Which A Number of Decisions Are Reached

Warren glanced down at his notes.
'We are concerned by your frequent misjudgments
of the surrounding reality and are recommending
a suitable course of treatment. As long as
dissident elements defend your cause, you are
a menace to society — and that means that legally
you are not accountable for your actions.'
Sheehan was taken from the room.

M ——, if
I speak, it is with the tongue of an insane man.
All truths are now silent. If I keep this silence
they will double their efforts to uncover a truth.
If I speak that truth, I will be silenced. How
am I cured of all this unknown wisdom? My tongue
removed that I may learn to speak?
S.

At five in the morning the ward lights flared.
Attendants dragged Sheehan from his mattress.
For ten minutes they forced him to dance.
Then one kneed him in the groin — made a loose
sack of his body. They pulled him to the end
of the room, where he was rolled tightly in
soaking sheets of canvas. They left him —
cigarette, cocoon — his body heat starting
the long process of evaporation.

❖

Warren was in his study, dangerously drunk; the file still open on his desk. 'My darling,' he said, 'Those who despise us so, who resent our inadequacies, who make us what we are for what they failed to be ——— . How often must we abide those faces turning away. Those who cannot realize how much we love, and pay for that love.' The telephone rang. Finchley was on the roof.

17 Finchley Goes Home

You have to surrender
to the getting wet. The danger of frosting slate.
The danger of coming down. But if you're *never*
coming down? The cold mucus damp came back again:
it was a game, through the mountains of a quilt.
The winter trees: hearts washed free of flesh,
albescent veins. He regretted the lack of training.
Someone else's choice to make him less than a man.
Not force on him the necessities: a returning
over the stumps, a through-vault, the left jab.
But slowly, by surrender, Finchley felt himself
clamber over the obstacle of his body, dragging
the sled-suitcase across the heights of St Clair.
Gymnasium. Sundial. All those familiarities lost
he'd thought in memory, encountered for this
first time in the lighting sky. He slid across
the wing, gargoyle-perched on the peak of an "A",
when he was blinded by light hissing full
in his face. The luggage abandoned on its slope,
careered into dawn. Thick ropes nudged him like
the snouts of attentive dogs. 'I've been very ill!'
he screamed. 'Yes, I was ill, yes! I didn't know
what I was doing when I did it!'

18 A Closing Incident

Who accuses us! Who dares
hold us responsible for that which we abhor.
Deprives us of our speech. Are we then to
be so utterly reduced — a cattle — in this
system that has no salvation, only retribution.
The blades of Warren's shadow scissored through
the corridors towards East Wing. Am I now
a stranger? Do I no longer have a sex? A self?
He paused against the turn. A darkened hall.
The light still pooling under Finchley's door.
'You bastard!' he cried, hurtling himself into
the room.
Finchley was clearly embarrassed by
the intrusion: half-naked, shivering, his hair
painted to his head. Warren brought him to
the ground with a single blow, relieved almost
with the absolute ease. Finchley rolled up
like a white caterpillar. 'Does this help?'
he screamed, slinging his boot into Finchley's
lower belly. 'You cunt! You fucking rich slit!
Does this make you feel better!'

19 Envoi

For the consequence of speech
there is no rest. These borders once again,
more familiar and unknown. This moment we are
the things he is — suffering these illnesses,
these deprivations, these human longings —
and the things that he may never be: a writer
and possessed.
Outside, a siren poem of the sane.
Each line abducted, turned against its brother.
Each line a forced betrayal. Our sight divided;
blinded by these endless thefts. Imaginations
turned to decorate the real!
And so we are
condemned for these "misjudgments of reality".
Our voices taken from us for the lie that
we have only dealt in lies.
My friends,
imprisoned with me in our different ways,
resist this murderous care, this history,
this false appropriation of the real!
Resist these poems! Their questions
and their sanity.
Their turpentine.
These guardians!
Resist these prohibitions of our speech!

RUN IN THE STOCKING

Bitter the knowledge we draw from voyaging!
Monotonous and mean, today, yesterday,
tomorrow, always, the world shows us our own
image — an oasis of horror in a desert of tedium.

Baudelaire

Prologue

Stormlight afternoon.
Backyards bleed together where fences have
long since fallen for winter heat. Two men
approach the cordoned soil with the resignation
of tent boxers. Janos lifts a masking sheet
of corrugated iron: stalks of pale green weed;
fingers of insects grasping for the dark —
clutching it from plant-shadow. A cold and
a damp. The men wield spades the toning of
their uniforms — like oceans taking colour
from the sky: diggers, in a version of day.
Their supervisor waits by the trees, amongst
fruit of fir and powder; leaves reduced by web.
He smokes, with a look of mild discomfort.
Their shovels grate through earth. An officer
already holds his breath: he knows the dangers
of inhaling vapors such as these. Then the
metal dies. They straighten. Jackson drops
and heels his cigarette. Here the soil goes
to sacking. Here to brown cotton flowers.
Here to half a jaw, eaten back to a grin.
But why, for a second, the toe-nails so near
the teeth? A shoulder bent this way, and legs
parcelled so contrary? Here the earth is
shimmering again. 'Steady!' says the supervisor.

They are in a cutting. The teacher draws
attention to a layer of flesh. Below, he notes,
the layer of rings. The layer of cosmetics
and of perfumed underwear. The supervisor
remembers muttering involuntarily 'We'll get
the bastard!' And the teacher saying 'This
is Geology. We don't kill in Geology, Jackson.'

And he replies eagerly 'But Sir, *I* know
who did it!'

He becomes aware of the long
dull hiss of leaves. Then a sudden wilfulness
of everything left unattached. A tearing at
the chains. Squib wind. But there is no storm.
Only these usual clouds. Only this industrial
light, and sun a distant warning. No storm.
Only this low lead sky, notched in the horizon
like the lid of a cauldron.

Part One
North

1

Dover woke to
his Doctor's French. The stainless steel clatter
of a ward at feeding time. That, and the face,
as if fingers — the slightly shifting fingers of
children playing statues — were against his skin.
'*Monsieur Andersson, j'ai plus de souvenirs, que
si j'avais mille ans.*' A laying on of hands. A fine
drizzle of touch.
'Baudelaire's *Spleen.* Of course,
by rights you shouldn't have *any.*' Their eyes met
over his wire spectacles. 'Memories. *I have more
memories than if I'd lived a thousand years.*
Do you know Baudelaire?' Mankevich burrowed in
his dressings. 'Seat of ill-humour and melancholy,
so they say. As in "a fit of spleen". "He gave vent
to his spleen" and so on.' A hectored ruddiness.
Thin lips. And above the lips a textureless moustache:
a carbon trail of flame on glass. 'Well now it's gone,
you should be equanimity itself!'

The railway yards
at dawn were a confluence of two blue-brown rivers.
A molten bruising, to and from the dole train.
Everywhere a vast impermanence. The milling rockets
of tents and clothes-sleds. Bicycles. Horses.
A collision of future and past. The Petro-void.
At the edge of this motion Dover held a match,

illuminating the government map. TURRET s391. The North had welcomed him with its blessing of compulsory transfer, a lifetime from that mortal sin. And that he should be shouldered by these men into an alley seemed the most tangible proof he was elsewhere.

The suitcase strap was cut; clothes exploded into flags. A pummelling against the face. He felt himself suddenly dream-light, flying above their heads, curving to a smooth and darkened lake. Then a rainbow from the downpour glass, a spread of warmth across the cheek; and only then that sharp intrusion through the gut. A damage had been done.

'Now we've had to do extensive facial work,' said Mankevich. 'Not much of a welcome North, I'm afraid.' His face emblazoned with the other cheek of medicine.

2

Dover's recovery seemed
an alcohol. The doctor swayed above his bed,
florid and short-breathed, the tiny red worms
floating to the surface of his cheeks.
'And whereabouts did you live in the South?'
That amorous concern with Dover's past;
with the laser tracings of face and belly.
Dover watched the doctor's red responding face
forever coming to the boil. 'Ah, physician heal
thyself!' said Mankevich. '*Acne Rosacea.*
Dilation of the superficial blood vessels —
chronic disease I'm afraid. Please go on . . .'
And Dover prattled on the surface of his past,
his tongue propelled by deeper images
he would never dare describe.

Yesterday
the exhumation. The worker's sudden pirouette
from the trench, caught on the jaw by a cloud
of decomposition. Today the autopsy. Today
a cataloguing of the limbs. Imprinted on the
marble eyes a likeness of her killer's face.
And when the face is punctured, and when the lips
are prised apart, the mouth in reflex spits
aloud the murderer's name.

'Mr Andersson?'
Dover fell back in bed. 'Perhaps I've over-

taxed you . . .' But Mankevich's short apology
was interrupted by a sudden clatter from
the end of the ward. Dover saw an aging man
restrained in white, in bed, and bellowing
in tongues; immodestly erect. The doctor's
eyebrows caught the nurse. 'Bile,' he said. 'Far
too much bile. Out with that liver tomorrow, eh!'

Dover walked for only a second time
into the Northern night.
Memories are waters boiling
with fish as the nets contract. A coming up
for air. A diving for water. Reliances. Animal
dependencies. He remembered. Once this was
called Sydney.

3

A blueprint from which no doubt
the South would rise, the accommodation towers
curved back into a scrim of air. Darker,
more satanic than his home.
Dover waited with
a dozen women for the elevator marked 27–40.
At 35 an old man entered, pulling a pram
in which, over piles of neatly folded clothes,
lay half a dozen seagulls. 'A flock, a whole
flock of 'em, lost their bearings,' he said,
laughing to himself. 'They come head first
into the laundry, silly buggers.' And for
a moment the pillowcase appeared to flap.
From the top floors the towers stuck through
the new atmosphere like mooring posts: mist
moving on the early surface of a lake.
Dover
stood upon the landing, upon stippled concrete
damp as a urinal floor. He feared most of all
a blow to the damaged gut, the spleenless gut,
for "cunts who'd do that to a woman!" But
the door swung harmlessly open and the lights
snapped on at their first detection of movement,
and he quietly walked in.
It was well before
the close of public lighting. Official night
that here began at ten. He unpacked what remained
of his belongings — thankful of the standard
compensation for compulsory moves — until he
found the photograph (insanity to bring it!
to carry that much of the South!) embedded in
the pocket of his overalls.
He saw her face,
her body, posed against the fig trees, reduced
to an Assyrian flatness. The coarse immensity
of chestnut hair, the prominent chin, the extreme
arch of her eyebrows. An elaborate high-necked

collar cutting at her throat. The image cutting at her waist: *Ingrid.*

He lowered himself onto the blankets and stared at the intricate bed-head carving: in this room a narrative on collective bargaining. Within three minutes he had moved so little that the lights expired. Dover stared into unwanted darkness. He knew some people purchased birds only for their constant movement; that their use was discouraged; and that many workers came home to find them dead — the room wreathed in a faint tincture of gas.

He flicked his leg, and the light returned.

4

Today a stranger's face, *unfastened in*
the waking world, becomes a permanence.
This ordinary look, distended by
regard — our brutal capability,
or what it realizes of itself —
accuses. Telling even here we are
no longer safe, nor any safe from us.

We learn the ruination of the love
of which we barely spoke, or scarcely touched;
the enervating repercussions of
that gentlest act, and this? A heart that beats
too quick, that raps for freedom of the past.
A life in fear of opening doors. That frame
and face; that mirrored truth of what we are.

5

Again this face.
Framed at the timber of an opened door. A view
that punctures like a bullet through the memory;
that burrows through the room; that tunnels
through the window to a neon, dull, extinguished
on a further terrace of the street.
A third night
sleepless, and another day in fear of sleep.
In the distant yard, a spade under weight of
the foot cuts through the sacking into her waist,
releasing its air. Someone vomits in reflex.
For the second time that month, Dover felt his
body piercing glass: his fist snapped through
the small square pane and ploughed against
EMERGENCY: a beginning and an end.
He squatted
next to the concrete pillar, his knuckles
smeared with blood, and watched as the horses
were released into the courtyard; as the tiny
bells of bicycles chirruped into evening shift.
And so the hour passed. An hour to arrive.
They took at least an hour.

There was a government
override on it anyway, so no investigation
was necessary. But something of the old school —
a nostalgia for investigation over clerkish
processing — took him. like a tourist through
the printout, ANDERSSON, DOVER. MALE. 35 . . .
the history of employment, transfer and assault.
Into the casbah of the out-clause: DEPRESSIVE
TENDENCIES. PREY TO MORBID FANTASIES. ENTRENCHED

GUILT PATTERNS LINKED TO EARLY DEATH OF MOTHER.
The Inspector hooked the elastic band from
underneath his chin, and placed his silver
cardboard hat upon the desk. He tossed back
the champagne and headed for the interview room.

❖

'Right. So they tell me you're a murderer.
Fair enough. I think probably all I need from
you at this stage is the body, a weapon and
a motive . . .'
As Dover gave his name and card,
embarking on confession, the Inspector felt
a seed wedged hard against his gum, in between
the top teeth. He pressed his tongue to the back
of his teeth and sucked violently. It made
a sound identical to that he used to talk
to his canary.
'. . . Just before I came here
from the South, I murdered a woman by the name
of Ingrid.'
'Yes?'
'I buried her. I buried
the body in a backyard of a house in Oakleigh.'
'Oakleigh.' He chirped three times. 'And you
don't recall her other name?'
'She never used it.
She was a prostitute.'
'A prostitute. In Oakleigh?'
A look of mild amusement rose to the surface
of the Inspector's face. 'Now you tell me why
you might have murdered this prostitute.'
'I don't remember. There are things I don't
remember . . .'
The Inspector picked up Dover's
security card and inserted it between his teeth.
'There could be others. I have this nightmare

of a man's face . . .'

The Inspector picked the seed from the corner of the card, along with a faint smear of blood. 'A man. When did these murders take place?'

'A month ago. That's why I came North.' The Inspector paused. 'Mr Andersson. I was under the impression you came North on a government factory permit.'

'That was luck. Coincidence.'

'Coincidence. Excuse me for one moment would you ...'

He stood, chirped once, and left the room.

6

Again Dover waited. Posing
for the camera. Guessing that his actions
whilst alone might somehow confirm a culpability.
He moved to the window and looked down.
Celebration. Independence Day for this year:
a mime ten floors below. He noticed a thumb-
print inside the double-glazing and felt that
sudden rush of irritation at poor workmanship.
Below, a dragon slowly coiled along the street.

He heard approaching footsteps, and the whistled
tune of *Happy Birthday*.
'Time to go home,'
said the Sergeant, holding open the door.
'I'm waiting for the Inspector.'
'Yes, well he's
busy right at the moment.'
'What about charges?'
'There's no charge. Our shout!' he said, enjoying
his quip as if it were a presage of promotion.
'You go home and have fun. Australia's ten today!'
He related this fact with a tenderness normally
reserved for only sons; and infected with a mild
remorse he put his arm around Dover's shoulder.
'There aren't any prostitutes in Oakleigh,
Mr Andersson. As far as we know, there isn't
any Oakleigh. Go home.'
On the way out, Dover
glimpsed the Inspector, two glass rooms away.
He was wearing a silver wizard's hat — champagne
in one hand, in the other a wand — trapped
halfway between drinking his health and making
him disappear.

❖

It was official night when Dover returned home, passing through that blanket of air, spiced with gunpowder. His flat remained in post-ten darkness.

Approaching the bedroom he became aware of the odour of soil; of the floor giving, spongelike, beneath his feet, like the uneven surface of a yard. He tried to regain the landing, but his legs gave out. His fall was broken by feather — a mattress of dead birds — gulls, their beaks cracked like china, necks snapped; smaller birds puffing gas. How many had he killed? Dover thrashed his arms. The lights came on. Six o'clock. Pillows, covers, damp. A door that opens on the truth of what we are.

He watched the first suggestion of day loosening the sky. Dover knew how any choice to travel is a form of suicide. Particularly South. Particularly now. And only for that face, perhaps he might have learnt to stay; and carried out the burden of her life to his own grave. But now, no choice.

It was time to go home.

Part Two
South

7

Everything runs away.
Down these slow inclines to a loneliness.
Streets, their drains, to which all water moves,
“finding its own level”. Driveways, gardens,
sloping away.

Dover fed into the queues of afternoon —
a shimmering of brown nylon jackets, the dullest
blue of overalls; myriad threads tied by the knot
of the station gates; the cold condensing marble
grace of its domes — every yard clutching his heart
for the packet of his settlement pay.
Until the train,
more like an insect now — if not for the speed,
then the spike and bristle of waving arms, tent poles:
the mass of workers spread across its roof —
crawled out through the turrets of civilization
to the first outposts: decentralized dole centres;
the carcass on which these flies would fall
and shift, blackening it, then swarming away,
with the sustenance of their month’s labour
and their government cash.
By eight, the train had
exchanged its first passengers, like filings
pulled and repelled by this dun-green magnet.

One-thirty. But smoke had reached them hours before.
Their throats grew scoured and conversation ceased.
They were a company of bandits; their handkerchiefs
water-soaked across the mouth. The train slid
through an orange after-fire glow. Cinders embedded
in their hair. Every minute workers crawled
exhausted from the roof, their faces piebald
with heat.

At the border to the South, Dover
left the crowds and dropped between the carriages:
his was a North and Northbound pass. The guards
cleared out compartments for the journey South and
hooded men sprayed the walls with antiseptic foam.
Then, as the latest unemployed moved in upon
the steaming wooden benches, and the stench
of phenol capitulated to the boiled-egg of steam,
sweat and poor diet, Dover clasped the handrails
of the inter-carriage walkway and swung back
to his seat.

By mid-afternoon, he watched
two massive blocks of blackened sky move together
like doors sliding along the horizon. Two blunt
hands that reached out to touch; two malignant
fleshes moving to collision and sutured by
a thread of lightning.

Shortly after came another

changing of the light; but more abysmal, thorough and unexpected. Sleeping and waking. The dull
lids closing over both.

8

Another waking, soaking, throttled
from the dream into the carriage's attention,
to what he thought must be the North again.
The train retreating through the massive
concrete pillars of residence. He slid his way
to the window.
He knew it must be dream.
Another dream — that nothing could have aged,
transformed the city in this space of weeks —
and here it must be somewhere else, except
the constant semi-mocking testimonies: 'It looks
like South to me!'
And now another voyage in
this unknown and populated space. And what
direction for this journey if all is known,
but unfamiliar? Who turns upon a continent
to explore if knowing this? Here so suddenly
mirrored with a Northern likeness. *What was
the meaning of this absent month?*
No cars —
their rusted and abandoned forms, like hedges
on the footpath's border — just these ubiquitous
electric tramcars, the bicycles, the horses.
A familiar geography, laced with its bitumen
grid, upon which another city had settled.

The tram at least still bore familiar numbers,
swaying, rolling down the inner streets.
A light diminished. Beige and stunted outcrops
he recalled as trees. Perhaps explosions in
the sulphur air?
He turned down the one-way

street (his wife, estranged these years)
towards the house. And yet no worker's art:
no recent pole-carving, but eroded work.
The painted footpaths and the gutters faded
to a pastel smear.
As he stood before the house
the curtains moved; an unknown face grown
fierce with fear appeared. The man was gesturing
as if to flick aside an insect; his voice
restrained by glass: 'You leave us be,' he said.
'You go back to your own area. We're not
looking for trouble.' The curtains closed, but only
momentarily. He reappeared behind the window
with a hammer. He pointed to it. 'You leave
us alone!' he screamed.

Outside the public house
the familiar HORSE FOR HIRE sign swung like
a guild marking. Dover made his way to the bar,
touching worker tile-paintings on the wall,
at last, with reassurance.
'Who do I see about
hiring a horse?'
'Where're you bound, mate?'
'Oakleigh.' The group of men surrounding
the transaction fell silent. Here would be
contested barter, amusement, or a fight.
'Now why would that be, mate?'
Dover turned
his face: an animal that wishes to submit.
'I'm sorry. I've been up North for a month.
Something's obviously happened.' The bar broke
into sudden laughter. 'Nothing's happened here
for fifty bloody years!' The bar burst out
again, and now everyone was wanting lines.
'Here Jim, make sure you get a decent deposit

on your pony. This bloke might decide he wants to settle down out there!'

But Dover had no humour now — his spleen, as it were, intact — and neither had the hirer. 'Two hundred. Plus Steve here goes with you — that's another hundred — to keep an eye on things. I wouldn't want to lose a good horse now, would I.' And virtually what cash remained, he offered for a bed that night in the hotel.

As he climbed the narrow staircase to his room, one of the men from the bar stopped him. 'Hey mate! You're a fuckin' idiot. You could've got that horse for a hundred!'

Dover mounted early in the morning. And with his unwanted Sancho, rode off in search of sanity.

9

And if all life should fall from earth
like angels, then the last remaining trace might be
these nets of road, these ribbons of a darker ash,
the deep-grey lines dividing waste. A sun-
of-sorts that trawled above an ocean glaze,
and air a visible darkness, as he galloped at
the edge of this bitumen scar.

The house was there.
Denuded of its timber, and the fences gone as in
his dreams of exhumation, but strangely old:
a friend diminished by disease, or pining
for a lover's death.
Only the Subsistant watched:
'Nothing here of use. She's not been treated
in years. That's dead soil.' Dover looked at
ashen earth and the ashen leaf of cabbages:
bent green arms, club-fisted with fruit the size
of brussels-sprouts. 'They're dead cabbages!'
Dover knew there was no body here — no soil had
turned within the month, or years — to hide, or
to discover. The watchman stood beside the horse,
distant, lighting a pipe. The horse, tied, still
snorting, to the white and rust of an abandoned
ice-cream van: a husk. Sans glass, sans wheels,
sans seat.
'This, around here's my run,' said
the Subsistant.
'How long's it been like this?'
'Since after the Towers,' replied the old man.
'Years.'
Dover wanted no more to pursue this

conversation now, than to have the moment of his death pronounced.

The Inspector's disbelief was all too clear, and the dreadful probability of madness crept into his understanding . . . the sanity he sought, smothered in the shedding
dusk of noon.

10

And so the lack of sleep
became a blessing — with this view an insect
burning in the eye — for as exhaustion spun across
his face, and fashioned packs of rifling labradors
from piled debris, the horse stampeded through
the stranger's door and rode into the room, hooves
battering the wooden boards. It reared, then
splintering the window panes, sprang into an explosion
of neon and bursting globes. Into the radiant
oblivion of TAMAT. Its resonance. Its holy sound.
This inadvertent utterance of the name of God.

At the eastern edge of tower-ring Dover,
hanging to another rein, gave back the
steaming, shining horse.
And now he stood,
back pressed to glass, for over fifteen
minutes in the booth, bound by the scepsis of this hope.
He touched for INFORMATION, and on request
hit NAME and keyed in TAMAT. The screen replied
precisely with its RESTAURANT and an address:
certificate of sanity. Certificate of death.

The tramcar stopped a hundred yards beyond
the restaurant. He felt conspicuous in his
worker's clothes, leaving at a stop so well
before his class. A bell rang and the patches
of the uniforms, adhering to end compartments

like counterweights, moved off into the dark. Dover stood beneath the sign; beneath its grey extinguished bulbs; then slowly turned to face the room. The window, one floor up, above a clothing store. Dover blessed his memory of the sign, and moving into TAMAT, spent his final dollars on a meal of dhal and puris.

As he ate he watched this window — rubbed only from his eye by passing trams, and the balanced cattle-weight of their illuminated workers, crashing towerwards.

He crossed the street and climbed the stairs which fed into a corridor.

Where this passage bluntly stopped, like an arm severed at the elbow, the dull nerve ends of Mrs Abbot scratched through evening. He watched the pen ineptly slotted in her hand: a beak preening the page. 'Hello?' he called.

'Terry?'

she cried, spinning round.

11

'No. Of course not. I'm sorry.
Can I help you?' Mrs Abbot raised a mitten hand
to his appearance, the arthritic fingers glued
into a solid flesh. 'My name is Dover Andersson.
I'm after the person who lives in the room . . .'
Her change of expression caused him to stop.
She cocked her ears like a dog will, hearing
the distant approach of its master. Then her face
seemed to topple into loose distress. 'He's dead.'
And Dover's face gave way along, and burst into
survivor's tears.

Mrs Abbot spread the
article upon her desk; pressed it flat the way
she might have smoothed a tablecloth. There had
been no immediate report — as if events
had fallen through a minute crack in time —
and this the only résumé. The headlines, even
with the respite of a week, were no less florid.
MARX AND MURDER. She read the article lovingly,
sipping hastily from her cup as if exalting in
the frequent sense of heat; turning her head
slightly: a swimmer in her tea.

The Philosopher Who Failed

'Come quickly, I've just killed Anne!' The scene and the suppliant, huddled and shivering despite the humidity of the Southern dawn were equally bizarre. Close by towered the stone walls and Gothic turrets of the 186-year-old University. The agitated man in robe and pyjamas banging at the door was no less notable: Terrence Rutherford, 35, among the diminishing survivors of this country's post-depression intellectual set and an academic star at the University. Answering the cry for help, the watchman discovered Rutherford's lover and fellow academic, Anne Morris, 30, dead on the bedroom floor at Rutherford's inner circle flat. An autopsy next day disclosed that she had indeed been murdered: her larynx was fractured and her thyroid gland damaged; common indications of strangulation. There were further signs of sexual assault. The tragedy however was not to stop there. For even as the watchman was examining the body, in an adjacent room Rutherford had taken his own life: ironically, hanging himself. In the time prior to the murder and suicide, Rutherford's intellectual credentials had come under critical scrutiny. Recent attacks on the government had become increasingly far-fetched and had contributed largely to an estrangement from his own party . . .

Mrs Abbot stopped. 'It had to happen while
I was away,' she said. 'The one time I'm away
with Sister Jess.'

The photograph of Rutherford —
that stranger — stared from the page. 'Have you
ever seen my face before?' asked Dover.

'No.'

'Then I was here when you were gone,' he said.

'And I saw Rutherford immediately before he died. I think I may have killed him.'

'Well, if you're a killer Mr Andersson,' she said without the slightest change in tone, 'You'll want to speak with Sandra Jones. She's the journalist who was interested in this case.' Then added conspiratorially: '*She* thinks that he was murdered too.'

12

He recounted. Absurdity.
Doubt. Vision. Dread. 'I am either a killer,
an agent, or a madman.' Knowing how to be
any of these would sew up this ragged world.
Sandra Jones leaned back in her chair. 'Then how
do I know whether I'm about to be murdered,
betrayed or simply confused!' And for the first
time Dover cried, crying for himself.

She brought tea.
'I knew Rutherford. Rutherford was brilliant.
He wasn't a murderer; and he held on to suicide
like a handstrap.'
Sitting forward, leaning back,
she used her hair like curtains, drawing them
against the closeness of a memory. And now
her face completely shaded as she poured: 'No one
even knew he was dead until *The Gazette* brought
out the resumé. *Fait accompli.* No last respects.
Another governmental override. The watchman gets
promoted from the public view . . .'

'He was
convinced this Government was using every
possible means to combat dissidence; that they
were capable of exceeding all bounds of propriety:
medical, psychological, under cover of emergency.
Then even his own people started to despair.

The more evidence he could supply — letters from
prisons, mental homes — the less they dared
believe him. The opposition here doesn't *oppose.*
Then adding as if she'd held this single
thought throughout: 'And I don't think you're
a murderer either.'
Dover felt something akin
to love for this woman that he knew he must
attribute first to tiredness, to expiation, or
to lust — or a dreadful need for anyone's belief.
'I'm the only one who does!' he said.

'Tell me
about Eltham.'
'It's a small, I suppose quite
wealthy area, linked by road to the north.
It's becoming isolated because of the petrol
problem. A lot of the richer people are starting
to sell and move closer in to the city . . .'

'Do you remember the first Tower being built?
Do you remember the Tower A17 disaster when
two hundred workers were killed or maimed?
Is this an accurate map of the safe beach areas?
How do you gain access to this area, here?
Tell me all you know about the Middle Circle.'

'I've never heard of it.'

Sandra Jones blew from her mouth. The curtains of her hair drew back. 'If you killed Terry Rutherford you did it by remote control. You haven't been here for over fifteen years!'

Part Three
North

13

But for the moment
that quilt of the old South lay before him.
'This was before zoning. They built a series
of ring towers around here.' She traced
a crescent round the city centre: a horseshoe,
its luck falling to the Bay. 'The Working Class
were compulsorily billeted in the towers;
unless they owned their own property, and
massive rating charges drove most of *them* out.
So the inner housing was swamped by the new
Middle Classes who'd dumped their outer-suburban
properties. A lot of them didn't make it ...
the towers are crammed with the downwardly mobile.
These areas here, the traditional pockets of
the rich, are now pass in/out areas: high-powered
residential, restricted access, and policed
twenty-four hours.'
The cane table was littered
with maps, clippings, concertina files, as Dover
slowly re-learned his city's history.

'Then where
did I get the image of the flat?'
'Coincidence?
A photograph somewhere? You've got two seconds
of anachronism inside a consistent pattern.
It's not much. I mean, are you *sure* it's exactly

the same? Did you go inside?'

'No.'

'By the way, while you were asleep this morning I had your security pass checked out by the best forger in the South — it's legal — so whoever you are, you're government approved. I was rather proud actually. It's the first investigative work I've done in years. Do you know what journalism is now? Stylistics. They told me in College that the role of the reporter is a chaperone for the reader on her first date with reality.' Dover rolled the bottle cork between his fingers, then snapped it in half. He stared at the layers, like a cutting: a layer of flesh, a layer of rings, a layer of cosmetics and of perfumed underwear.

❖

Whilst undressing she forced herself to recognize the stigma of her nipples: growing inwards. Never 'sleepy' but belligerent. Burrows of indecent animals that bred inside her breasts. And in return the luxury of accidentally touching herself; the shock of finding herself wet, as if a thought had been with her longer than she knew.

And something like the way she felt that Rutherford might be, have been, apart from Anne, diminished in efficiency and nightgowns; and the nagging fear of what this strangest man might represent.

Finally, within her bed, that with her celibacy, these feelings were at best worthy of a brief analysis; at worst, irrelevant.

She lay in that bed, hearing his sleep-ridden cries from the other room, garbled and erratic. "A long journey tomorrow," she thought. She imagined her father come into the room — "my brilliant and beautiful father" — Head of the Department of Mathematics; "who thought himself to death without me." She remembered his "nursery rhymes". How he'd sit at the end of her bed, and she'd smell his opened briefcase, and he would sing. She heard her father softly singing 'In any right-angled triangle, the square of the hypotenuse is equal to the sum of the squares of the other two sides.' The world took men from her, like a tithe.

The interstate express that carried Jones into the North, roared past the endless dole-trains, waiting, cowered in their sidings.

Before another bedtime she visited a public phone and rang Dover at her flat. 'I'm here. Call me at the number I gave you from a public box. 19.30 exactly. I'm off to hospital tomorrow.' 'Be careful!' he said. A line for which she had no reply.

14

The nurse asked Dover to step back into the surgery. 'Mr Andersson,' said the doctor, 'You *did* say you'd been in hospital for removal of the spleen?... Yes, I thought so. Well I'm afraid your spleen is still very much there. You've been broken into as it were, but nothing's been taken! According to the scan the only thing you've lost is your looks: you're carrying around some of the most advanced facial modelling I've seen.' Dover laughed.

The globes surrounding TAMAT were dull and grey. Burst. Opened like strange tulips.

'No, no trouble, Mr Andersson,' said Mrs Abbot. 'I've been expecting you. The room is still the same. I'll not be the one to change things. How is Sandra keeping?'

Dover let the door swing back. But rather the insanity of re-enactment: an accusation of the now decaying Rutherford propped in his frame than what he saw. There was no face. No window. No view across the room towards the dull TAMAT. And if not here, then where could he ever find this unnamed guilt.

Inside the room he calmed; quietly
reconstructing the geometries of where this view
might coincide. Until he understood.
The frame
was not a door frame, but another darker timber.
He slowly drew himself towards the dressing table.
There. A reflection of bulbs and the palindromic
sign of TAMAT; and his own face looking in
this mirror where another's must have been.
Unless. His memory seemed held up to the light.
That frailest of objects, that tissue, with
its single pin-prick hole, that suddenly was
pulled apart around the room.

The first two
men who entered, held him; forcing him to
watch the sexual violation of his lover. Then
the second two men held him, as he watched
her throttled and the quick release of sperm
that shuddered down her broken throat; and one
who turned to him and said 'Of course we're
not really doing this. *You're* doing it.
We're simply ignorant men creating history,
Doctor Rutherford.' And his face turned and
stared into the mirror of the nightmare.

Where he now stood.
Dover walked back slowly
from the room, across the hurdles of its
books and serials. Between the armchairs, shrouded
in their double sheets.
'They killed her,'

he said, 'And I'm alive.' Mrs Abbot stood before him holding a gun. 'You take this. It's a bit beyond me now. Take it. You don't tackle these people unarmed!' she said, adding,

'Now best I explain how to use it.'

15

The telephone rang
only twice before she answered. 'Dover?'

'Yes.'

'I hope you're ready for some willing suspension of disbelief. I got to the main files on a bogus feature. Mr Dover Andersson left the hospital on the fourteenth of February. Only trouble is that according to the records he was never admitted. I've been given the name of a sympathetic orderly; I need to get something more specific on these operations . . .'

'I've already been to a doctor,' said Dover. 'I never had the spleen removed. Only my face.'

'Well I'm not sure who you are, but it looks like Dover Andersson's not a good choice.' '*I* know who I am,' he said. 'I'm Terry Rutherford.'

Dover pulled the book of Baudelaire from Jones' shelf and settled back into the chair. An hour later he knew his heart exploding. Reading. From this patchwork quilt of past, Dover recognized the fabric of his waking dream: the supervisor sewn across another's sky. Mankevich's love of Baudelaire smeared inside the roof of his skull: *the terror of the freethinker, the hope of the crazed hermit — the sky, the black lid of the cauldron wherein mankind boils, vast and insignificant.*

Sandra Jones, journalist, stood before the screen as Dover's "life" flashed before her eyes. Each micro-print that weeks before replaced the self of Rutherford. She switched it off. She pictured the man in her flat. What could she now love: who did not look like "he"; who could not think like "he"; but who *was* "he". And for whom had she felt that moment of attraction? The door behind her opened.

Another hour passed.

No answer. Dover left the public phone, deciding to return and cook a meal. Like his settlement of days before, each yard he gently slapped the gun inside his coat.

As he turned the corner he saw the government vehicles whine to a halt outside her flat. He watched as three men emerged. A guard plugged the vehicles into recharging posts. He watched the lights go on upstairs. He watched the shadows thrown across the blind like "truth".

It was time to go home.

16

North.
The pulsing sky had lowered itself to just above
the face: every building now a fallen monolith;
columns of the tower-blocks reduced once more
to concrete plinths.
Dover watched pedestrians
materialize amongst this drizzle; their varied
paths amalgamated by the lack of definition to
a constant vigilance.
He climbed the hospital steps.
Here a pair of spectacles; these two round mirrors,
one lens cracked: a bicycle. And at the corner of
his eye a pram descending unattended. Its nurse
abducted by another's sight.
He entered the foyer,
making his way to *Reception.* 'My name is Dover
Andersson. I was discharged from this hospital
two weeks ago. I've been having recurrent headaches,
hallucinations. I'm finding it impossible to work.'
'Andersson?' she asked, turning to the keyboard.
A pause. 'Just take a seat would you Mr Andersson.'
And as he sat he once again rehearsed his unlived
days inside the tower flat; until a voice swerved
in between the milling groups of visitors and
a reddened polished face bobbed to a halt against
his side. 'Ah, Monsieur Andersson. Headaches is it!
The groaning mind tortured by long-felt cares.'

By now he knew their movements well enough.
Waiting until late in the evening shift, Dover
slipped from the private room and starting with
the wing in which he had been placed, secreted

from the ministrations to the proper ill, he searched.
When Dover saw her — Sandra — through the small
square viewing window, he felt that half-formed love;
until he wondered what of him was loving her. If not
the eyes of Rutherford, perhaps the lust of Mankevich.
'Are you alright?' he asked. She stared at him
from the bed, stiffening, drawing the clothes
higher to her chin. 'Yes?' she said, tentatively.
He could see her mounting anxiety. She didn't know
him. Had never seen him before, this worker.
Whoever she now was, whose face alone remained
this long.

And as he stood, the door swung wide.
And Dover recognized another face.

17

'When shall we three meet again?
Hello Terry.' The bound chestnut hair, dragged
from the forehead: a hood about her face.
The half-closed eyes; their deep belongings
to rapture. A white coat buttoned high at
the neck.

'Hello Ingrid.'

'Judith. Judith
Anders.' And held out her hand. 'Ingrid was
from a very old film.'

And so the faces that
he knew in dream were reassembled in this
waking world. He had seen her broken, dis-
assembled beneath his gaze, who was now whole,
and animate again.

'You really weren't
supposed to ever go South again, you know.
What was it?'

'My own face, accusing me.'
'Just that slightest trace of past,' she mused.
'What amazing resilience. It's the same rat
that survives the holocaust. I'm sorry. How
was the South. I've not been there for …'
'Fifteen years.'

'Yes.'

'It's changed. Where
you remembered suburbs, there's only desert.
The fields are gone. It's all ash now, this
Oakleigh. A "desert of tedium" as it were.
Much like here.'

'I did want you to have some
sweets with all your trouble.'

'Some poetry?'
'Oh, I found the Baudelaire a lovely touch.
Mankevich suggested it. He's very fond of
Baudelaire. And as for killing me — and me
a most ignoble prostitute — a little irony

there for both of us. I forget, did we programme in my speciality? Her total love of domination. I fancy this creature hated herself to do all those things. You were a most engaging jigsaw, Terry.'

'My God,' said Dover, racked within this newest conscience. 'Why didn't you simply kill him.'

18

A look of indignation spread across
her face. 'Kill you! Because I don't have
the power of life and death. That's for God,
and for thugs. You know what society demands,
if we are going to survive this stupid present.
It demands respect and obedience. It demands
above all the humane elimination of everything
that represents or might occasion change —
by which I mean unwanted or unplanned disruption.
This society demands punishment. The masses
demand it for their murderers and their thieves.
We for those who stand in the way of this
unpleasant but necessary crawl back to civilization.
So we punish you with these guilts, and with
these nightmares — which is more 'humane' than
execution; more clean and expedient, more
economical than a life behind bars. But you
will have forgotten the simple tortures
available to a man armed with a cola bottle,
let alone with water, rags and a cigarette.
We give you a meaningful job in our factories,
and you are rehabilitated, and amongst us;
unrecognized with your new face and your
new past, but a free being, making these amends
within yourself.'

Dover took the borrowed gun
from his pocket, firing twice, then four more
times into her gut. He saw the last expression
on her face: not as he had dreamt it, but a look
of disappointment.

He saw Sandra Jones, or
whoever she now might be, run from the bed,
the room, hysterically, down the corridor
calling for help. He sat down against the
metal cabinet and drew Anders close to his side.
'Ingrid,' he said, 'you cannot hope to understand
the guilt I've felt for killing you. You cannot

hope to understand how liberating it is to find
that I have never killed.'
                                        One leg was bent
beneath her, contrary, and broken by her own fall.
Her stocking had caught on the bedside and
laddered badly. A hole like a pale flattened ball;
and behind it endless crescents: the shockwaves
      of its impact.

COPYRIGHT

First published in 1986 by University of Queensland Press.

This edition published in 2021 by Ligature Pty Limited
34 Campbell St · Balmain NSW 2041 Australia
www.ligatu.re · mail@ligatu.re

e-book ISBN: 9781922749062

ligature untapped

This print edition published in collaboration with Brio Books, an imprint of Booktopia Group Ltd

Level 6, 1A Homebush Bay Drive · Rhodes NSW 2138 · Australia

Print ISBN: 9781761281488

briobooks.com.au

MIX
Paper from responsible sources
FSC® C008194

The paper in this book is FSC® certified. FSC® promotes environmentally responsible, socially beneficial and economically viable management of the world's forests.